how to build boat trailers

by GLEN L. WITT

Second Edition

marine GLEN designs

Library of Congress

Witt, Glen L.
   How to Build Boat Trailers, 2nd Edition/Glen L. Witt
   Rev. ed. of: How to Build boat Trailers. 1982.
   Includes supplier list and index.
   ISBN 0-939070-08-1
                                                96-094859
                                                CIP

Questions regarding the ordering of this book or any other GLEN-L publication should be addressed to:

GLEN-L marine designs
9152 Rosecrans Aveue
Bellflower, CA 90706-2138

about this book...........

We've tried to make this book reader friendly. The type was selected for readability of style and size. Page numbers are indicated with bold oversize numerals on the bottom outside corner. The name and number of each chapter is on the outside upper corner of facing pages. Section contents are noted in large bold type. Drawings and photos are indicated by Chapter number followed by another number e.g., FIG. 5-3 would be the third drawing or photo in Chapter 5. A Table of Contents lists Chapter heading by page number. The Index provides quick page number access to a given subject.

acknowledgments..........

A book such as <u>how to build boat trailers</u> would not be possible without the valuable assistance of many companies and their informative representatives. Many of the drawings, details, and photos in this book were furnished by these helpful organizations. We thank them very much. We've tried to give credit to all the suppliers who furnished pictures or drawings of their products. If we missed any it was by accident. A list of source addresses is given in the appendix.

Thanks also to TRAILER BOAT MAGAZINE. Over the years they have run numerous articles on boat trailering that have been a help writing this book.

And a special thanks to the GLEN-L staff who tolerated the many moods of this writer and who had the tedious task of reading... and re-reading the manuscript.

Table of Contents

INTRODUCTION

The discussions that follow will cover the construction of boat trailers intended for transporting boats that fall within the standard trailerable width as defined by state and federal regulations. Such trailers will usually be limited to carrying boats under 30' in overall length, as boats longer than this are seldom under the maximum trailerable width. The text will cover trailer construction from the undercarriage through the frame, as well as the various appendages such as trailer hitches, lighting, and forms. There is also general information valuable to anyone desiring to trail a boat.

Most commercially built trailers are quality products. The trailer manufacturers, however, must attempt to build a trailer that will fit as many types and sizes of boats as possible. The individual building his own trailer builds it to fit his particular boat. It is a custom-fitted, balanced unit, with features needed to accommodate prevailing conditions in the particular area where the boat will be trailered and launched. This text will also prove valuable to the individual who wishes to purchase a manufactured trailer. It will enable him to determine what modifications will be practical for his boat, and the various suggestions should make trailering a boat more pleasurable.

The most common type of boat trailer used today is the standard single axle, two-wheeled trailer. For the larger boats, the tandem axle trailer is more common. The four-wheel type trailer with two axles, one at each end, is seldom used as it is awkward to handle, and with current heavy-duty undercarriages, larger boats can be trailed on a tandem wheel-type trailer.

A trailered boat usually spends more time in storage on the trailer than in the water. The trailering of the boat to and from the water will probably be harder on the structure of the boat than the actual usage when afloat. A good trailer duplicates, as much as possible, the same support given the boat when in the water. The trailer must be long enough to fit the boat and support it from transom to stem. The hull should be firmly supported through the forms to the chassis and provide a firm, non-flexing support.

The entire rig must be balanced, and of a capacity to carry the boat and all accessories that are likely to be stored or trailed in the boat. The balance of the trailer and boat plus load is all important. Improper weight on the tongue of the towing vehicle may cause dangerous trailer sway or bounce. The properly equipped, designed, and balanced trailer will tow evenly and smoothly and make launching the boat and the retrieval easy and simple. It will be easily maneuvered by the towing vehicle, and simple to attach and uncouple. When uncoupled, it should be possible to move the trailer and boat to the parking or storage area without undue effort.

how to build boat trailers

YOUR TRAILER AND THE LAW

Both federal and state governments have rules and regulations for boat trailers as do some of the boating industry groups. However, as of this writing there isn't a uniform set of regulations that apply to all states.

A prime example is trailerable widths without a "wide load" permit. Maximum trailerable width in the past has been 8'. This was changed by the Federal government to 8' 6" but in the workings of the bureaucracy, not all states adopted this as law. It is our understanding that funds are or will be withheld from states not conforming to the greater width limitations to force compliance of this regulation. However, at this time a few states do not allow trailers over 8' without special permits.

A license plate is currently required for all trailers operating on the highways. Unfortunately, uniformity on other requirements is lacking. Thus, prior to trailering a boat, check all applicable state regulations, and those of other states you may wish to trail your boat to or through.

"TRAILER BOATS" magazine in Carson, California has done an exceptional job of publishing trailering requirements for each state. This is currently published at the first of each year and is an excellent reference. ❖

AXLES

The axle (or axles) of a trailer is the main horizontal bar that supports the downward load from the frame and the boat being carried. It must also keep the spindles on each end of the axle in alignment. Spindles in turn support the bearings and hubs that are bolted to the wheel.

Axles for leaf or coiled springs are available in two types, either straight or dropped. The straight axle is level from spindle to spindle with the exception of the provisions for camber. The drop type dips down from the spindles on either end enabling the springs, and thus the chassis and the load, to be lower to the ground. Axle drops of 2" to 6" in 2" increments are standard with most manufacturers.

Axles come in a variety of shapes: solid rectangular, round, or "I" section and tubular round, square or rectangular. Although separate spindles can be obtained from manufacturers and welded to tubular or round sections, this is probably not the most practical method for obtaining an axle. The big problem is determining the capacity of the fabricated axle. Most often this is a "by guess and by gosh" method at best. The result is an axle that is either much stronger than required and thus heavy, or one that is under strength and dangerous to use. The manufactured type of axle is by far the most satisfactory in the long run and will usually be very close in cost to the one the individual would attempt to make. The

manufactured axle are available in a various sizes, capacities, and overall or track widths. Manufacturers will supply the load capacity of their axles; some will have a plate attached that furnishes such information.

Let's analyze the term "load capacity"- the practical load the axle will carry with a factor of safety included. This does not mean a 2000 lb. rated axle will carry a 2000 lb. boat. The load capacity is total weight that can be carried and must include the weight of the trailer frame. And while you're at it, don't forget all the junk you or the family may carry in the boat.

Axles can be attached directly to the frame. This will beat the boat to a pulp and is impractical for road worthy trailering. The most common suspension method is to cushion the axle from the frame with springs; coil or most commonly, leaf type. The closer the springs are mounted to the wheels, the less deflection in the axle. Most trailer axle manufacturers specify the capacity of the axle with varying distances between the tire centerline and spring centerline. As a general rule, mount the springs as close as practical to the wheel of the trailer. The advantage of this will be obvious in the following example of a prominent manufacturer. This manufacturer rates a 1 3/4" square axle at 3000 lbs. capacity. If the distance from tire to spring centerlines (overhang) is 9 1/2", the axle will actually have a capacity of 3120 lbs. If,

how to build boat trailers

SINGLE AND MULTIPLE AXLE TRAILERS

FIG. 2-1: Boat trailers may have one, two, or three axles. Most boats can be carried on trailers with one or two axles. Larger and heavier boats may require three axles to carry the required load. Courtesy "TRAIL RITE"

TRAILER AXLE CAPACITY

Beam Selection Procedure: Determine overhang = Distance from center of spring to center of tire. Select axle size from chart.

AXLE BEAM		1 1/4" SQ.	1 1/2" SQ.	1 3/4" SQ.	2" SQ.	SUPREME	2 1/4" SQ.	2 1/2" SQ.	3" SQ.
CROSS SECTION									
SECTION MODULUS		0.325	0.562	0.893	1.33	1.36	1.9	2.6	4.5
WEIGHT PER FOOT		5.31	7.65	10.4	13.6	12.8	17.2	21.2	30.6
O	7	1205	2460	4230	6510	6820	9780	13300	22900
	7 1/2	1125	2290	3950	6070	6360	9030	12400	21400
	8	1055	2150	3700	5690	5970	8470	11600	20050
	8 1/2	995	2020	3490	5360	5620	7970	10900	18850
V	9	940	1910	3290	5060	5300	7530	10300	17800
	9 1/2	890	1810	3120	4800	5020	7140	9780	16850
	10	845	1720	2960	4550	4770	6780	9280	16000
	10 1/2	805	1635	2820	4330	4540	6450	8850	15250
E	11	770	1560	2700	4140	4350	6150	8440	14600
	11 1/2	735	1495	2580	3960	4170	5880	8080	14000
	12	705	1430	2470	3790	3990	5640	7740	13400
	12 1/2	675	1375	2360	3640	3830	5420	7430	12850
R	13	650	1320	2270	3500	3680	5210	7140	12350
	13 1/2	625	1270	2190	3370	3540	5010	6880	11900
	14	605	1225	2110	3250	3410	4840	6630	11480
	14 1/2	585	1185	2040	3140	3290	4670	6400	11090
H	15	565	1145	1970	3040	3180	4520	6190	10720
	15 1/2	545	1110	1910	2940	3080	4370	5980	10370
	16	525	1075	1850	2850	2980	4230	5800	10040
	16 1/2	510	1040	1790	2760	2890	4100	5630	9730
A	17	495	1010	1740	2680	2800	3980	5470	9440
	17 1/2	480	980	1690	2600	2720	3870	5310	9170
	18	465	955	1640	2530	2650	3760	5160	8920
	18 1/2	455	930	1600	2460	2580	3660	5020	8680
N	19	445	905	1560	2400	2510	3560	4880	8450
	19 1/2	435	880	1520	2340	2450	3470	4760	8230
	20	425	860	1480	2280	2390	3390	4640	8020
	20 1/2		840	1440	2220	2330	3310	4530	7820
	21		820	1400	2170	2270	3230	4420	7630
	21 1/2			1370	2120	2220	3150	4320	7450
G	22			1340	2070	2170	3080	4220	7280
	22 1/2			1310	2020	2120	3010	4130	7120

FIG. 2-2: This chart represents the effect of overhang (the distance between leaf spring centers and the track) on the capacity of an axle. These figures are for use comparatively and not as a criteria for all axles of comparable size.

how to build boat trailers

however, the overhang is increased to 12", the capacity decreases to 2470 lbs. If the overhang is further increased to 20", the capacity would drop to a very low 1480 lbs. usable capacity even though the actual rating of the axle would still be 3000 lbs. The figures just noted do not necessarily apply to all 1 3/4" axles. They are cited as examples to indicate the importance of spring location relative to that of the tire and wheel.

When ordering a trailer axle, consideration must be given to whether trailer brakes are to be used; brakes will be discussed in detail in Chapter 6. Brake flanges are available on manufactured trailer axles at minimal cost. They must, however, be ordered with the axle if brakes are to be utilized.

Smaller boat trailers use single axles, while heavier ones may use two or even three to provide the total capacity required. Tandem axle trailers provide a smoother ride as the load is spread over more support points, and are usually less prone to fishtail than single axle types. Wheel diameter can also be reduced on a tandem trailer. The lower center of gravity makes a blowout less likely to cause serious damage. In the absence of a spare, it is also possible to come home on three wheels by removing the tire and lashing the hub to the frame...but only if you drive very slowly. Tandems, however, have more components, cost more, and require additional maintenance. They tend to track in a straight line, and maneuvering an uncoupled trailer is more difficult. Most experts

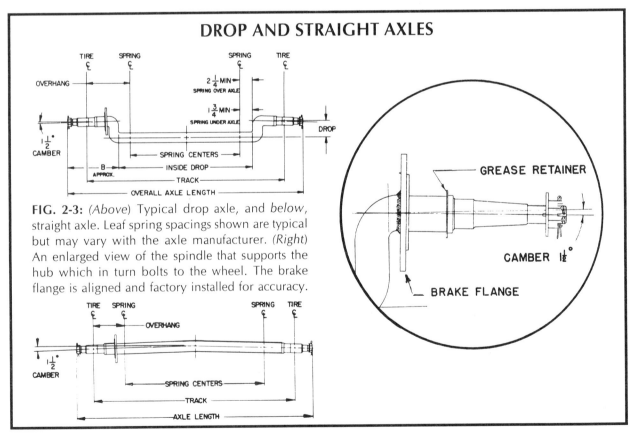

DROP AND STRAIGHT AXLES

FIG. 2-3: *(Above)* Typical drop axle, and *below,* straight axle. Leaf spring spacings shown are typical but may vary with the axle manufacturer. *(Right)* An enlarged view of the spindle that supports the hub which in turn bolts to the wheel. The brake flange is aligned and factory installed for accuracy.

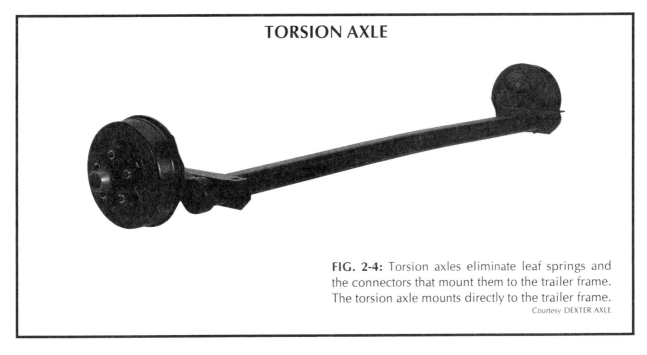

TORSION AXLE

FIG. 2-4: Torsion axles eliminate leaf springs and the connectors that mount them to the trailer frame. The torsion axle mounts directly to the trailer frame.
Courtesy DEXTER AXLE

feel that tandem axle trailers are best for boats in the 2500 lb. or more range.

TORSION AXLES AND SUSPENSION SYSTEM

Torsion bar axles are a complete suspension system. They are totally self-contained and eliminate the need for leaf or other type of spring suspension (see Chapter 3). A torsion bar axle system suspends the spindles and wheels on a short trailing crank arm that pivots around or in a cross bar housing that could be called the axle. However, torsion axles need not extend from wheel to wheel; they may be separate independent units, one for each wheel. When torsion axles do not extend completely across the frame, considerable twisting action takes place. A trailer frame member located adjacent to the torsion axle mounting is therefore advised.

Resistance to pivoting of the arm about the housing is usually provided by rubber mounting or steel spring methods. This resistance to twisting between the arm and housing is torsion; hence the name of the system.

Torsion axles are selected to accommodate the weight of the load to be carried. Most will carry a range of loads: 2500 to 3500 lbs., 3600 to 6000 lbs., etc. are typical examples. Each wheel of a torsion system functions independently. The wheels and trailing arms move up and down and rotate the torsion bars which absorb the motion caused by road conditions. Each wheel rides independently over road bumps. Since the torsion system is mounted directly to the frame, much of the side sway, common with leaf springs, is eliminated. The torsion axle system does not drop down when unloaded as much as a spring leaf system. Ground clearance can be lessened as the torsion system mounts directly to the trailer frame.

how to build boat trailers

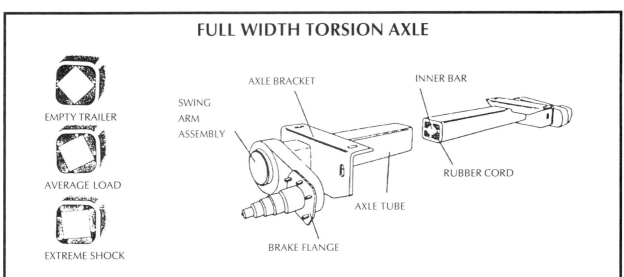

FULL WIDTH TORSION AXLE

EMPTY TRAILER

AVERAGE LOAD

EXTREME SHOCK

SWING ARM ASSEMBLY

AXLE BRACKET

INNER BAR

RUBBER CORD

AXLE TUBE

BRAKE FLANGE

FIG. 2-5: This torsion system uses an inner metal bar with four rubber cords encased in an outer axle tube. The arm assembly pivots inside and utilizes the natural torque action of the rubber cords to provide a superior ride. The axle is easily mounted on the trailer frame with only four bolts and forms a cross beam on the trailer frame. *(Left)* Section drawings, taken through the axle, illustrate the torsion forces imposed by the swing action of the arm supporting the wheels under average, no load, and extreme load conditions.

Courtesy HAYES AXLE, INC.

Torsion axle systems are more costly than conventional axle/leaf springs, however, they eliminate the many components required. Rubber, such as used in most torsion axles, can be temperature sensitive and may deteriorate in time. If water, particularly saltwater, gets into a torsion system that is not galvanized or otherwise protected, corrosion can develop. However, the torsion system has been used much longer in Europe than in the US. with good results. Still, checking with the supplier of these units and determining their solution to these problems should be considered, particularly if the trailer is to be submerged during boat launching.

SPINDLES

A spindle is a machined portion at either end of an axle to support the bearing races of the hub. Spindles are precisely machined so the bearings slide on easily, but with a snug fit. If a bearing doesn't slip over the spindle readily, don't get out the hammer. Rather, check for even the slightest burr that may be left after machining and remove with sandpaper or file; just remove the burr, don't sand or file the spindle bearing surfaces. Wipe clean with solvent and the bearing will probably slip on easily. ❖

SPRINGS

Springs for trailers may be coil, leaf, torsion, or pneumatic. For most applications the leaf spring is the best choice for the individual building his own boat trailer. They are commonly available, and their simplicity of installation as well as their ease of maintenance makes them ideal for all types of boat trailers.

Just as with all of the other components of the trailer, the springs have a capacity limitation. Springs are rated for a certain load per set or per each. A spring that has a greater load applied than intended may bottom or fail in use. One that has a much greater load capacity than it is carrying will tend to make the suspension stiff. This, then, makes for a harder riding rig that will transmit road shocks to the boat being carried. Salvaged springs obtained from an auto wrecking yard can be used, however, unless the capacity of the springs is known, they are difficult to match to the load requirements for trailer use.

The standard leaf spring is basically a single spring steel flat bar bent into an arc with an eye and bushing on either end. Originally developed for automobiles, it was readily adaptable to early trailers and has stayed on as a practical suspension system. The standard two eye trailer spring will have an eye to eye dimension of 26".

Slipper springs are somewhat cheaper than the standard two eye spring. One end of the top leaf of a slipper spring is flattened and slides in a tubular sleeve or similar device welded to the trailer frame. A standard trailer slipper spring will have an overall length eye to slipper end of 25".

SINGLE AXLE SPRINGS

The principle of the leaf spring is the same whether using the standard two eye or slipper type. Additional leaves are added to the spring to gain strength, as seldom will a single spring leaf be adequate. The springs are held together in the center by a bolt or pin through all of the leaves. At the outer extremities, a "U" shaped fitting holds the springs together so they will not shift from side to side.

The assembled leaf springs are mounted to the axle by "U" bolts as shown in FIG. 3-1A. A plate (FIG. 3-1F) holds the spring to the axle, in conjunction with "U" bolts. The plate has a hole recessed in the center to accommodate the bolt used to hold the spring leaves together. It is also necessary to have a counter-drilled hole in the axle to accommodate the other end of the bolt holding the leaves of the spring together. A plate or other type of spring landing on the axle is also common. The "U" bolts holding the springs to the axle should be equipped with lock washers and securely tightened.

15

how to build boat trailers

LEAF SPRING ASSEMBLIES

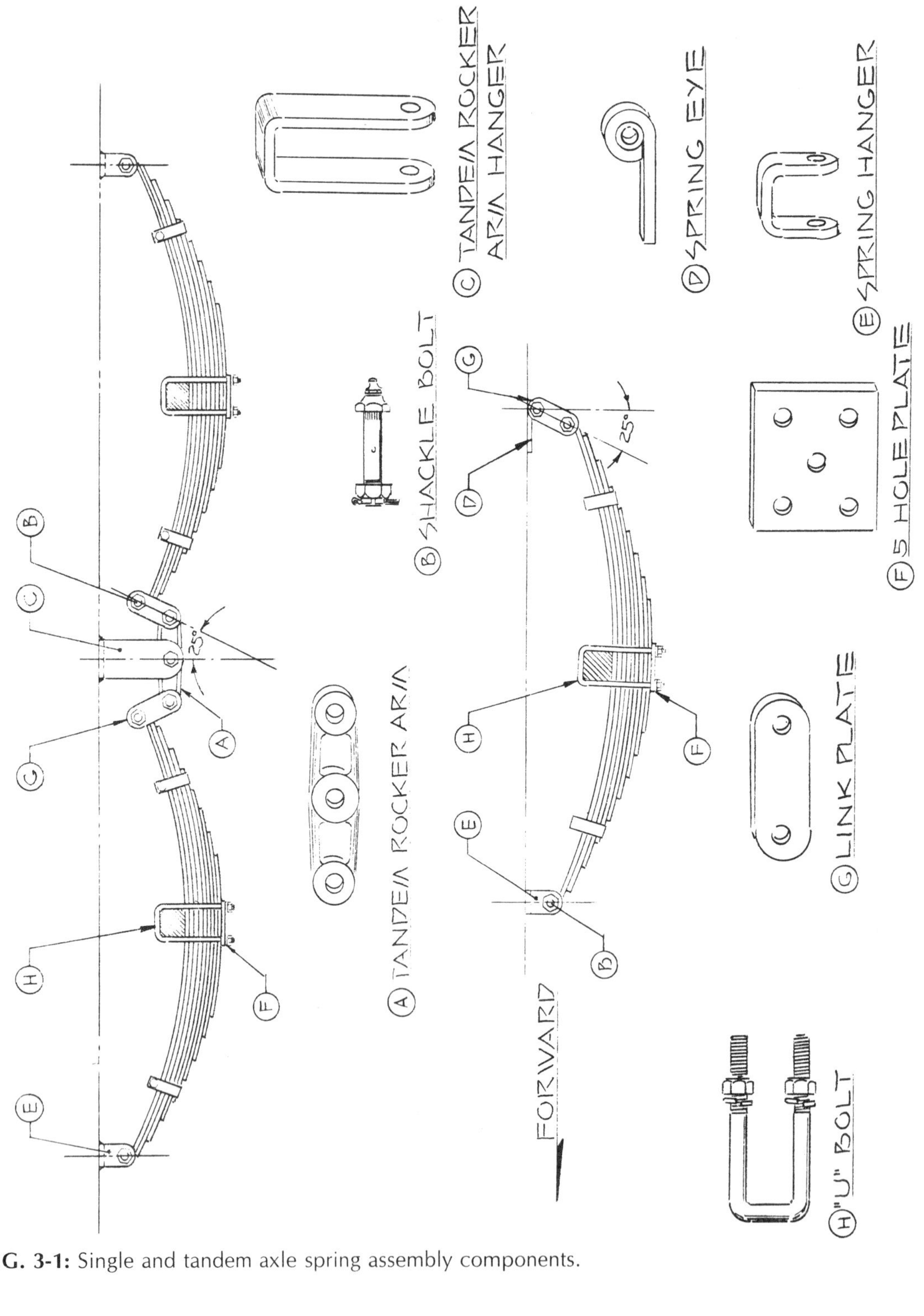

FIG. 3-1: Single and tandem axle spring assembly components.

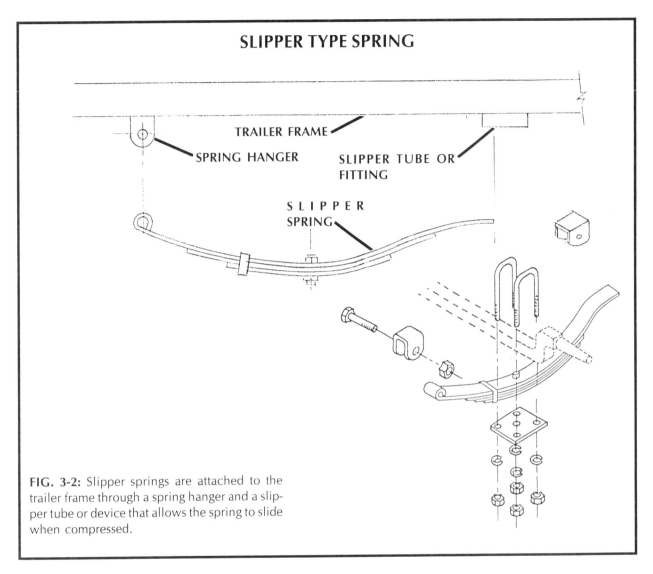

SLIPPER TYPE SPRING

TRAILER FRAME

SPRING HANGER

SLIPPER TUBE OR FITTING

S L I P P E R SPRING

FIG. 3-2: Slipper springs are attached to the trailer frame through a spring hanger and a slipper tube or device that allows the spring to slide when compressed.

Although the leaf spring shown in FIG. 3-1 illustrates the axle above the spring, the reverse is possible. The axle below the spring is sometimes necessary to provide proper height for road clearance, or to raise the frame when the boat is intended to ride over the wheels.

A hanger is welded to the trailer frame at the forward end of the standard double eye spring. A shackle bolt holds the spring to the eye with a bushing, usually of bronze. An eye is welded to the trailer frame or supporting member for the other end of the spring. From this eye, two link plates (FIG. 3-1G) connect the spring to the eye (FIG. 3-1D). Shackle bolts are used at either end of the link plates, extending through the spring eyes and bushing in the leaf spring. The shackle bolt is locked with a cotter key and equipped with a lubrication fitting on one end to grease the pivoting bushing. The link plates connecting the spring to the eye are canted at approximately a 25 degree angle to

17

provide free movement as flexing occurs.

TANDEM AXLE SPRINGS

Tandem assemblies can be rigged in several ways; however, the one shown in FIG. 3-1 is possibly the most common. This system is similar to the assembly for single axles with the exception of the longer tandem rocker arm hanger and the tandem rocker arm connecting link plates to each of the springs. Again, note the angularity of 25 degrees used at the center spring mounting to provide free movement of the assembly.

TRAILER BALANCE

Adjusting the balance of a trailer is easily done if leaf spring assemblies are attached to steel

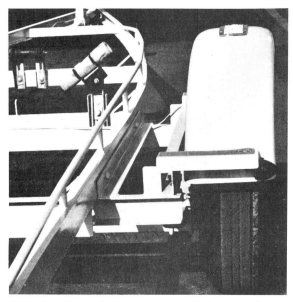

FIG. 3-4: Spring/axle mounting method similar to that shown in FIG. 3-3, except the springs are mounted on athwartship members; these in turn are mounted to angle longitudinals that fasten to the trailer frame.

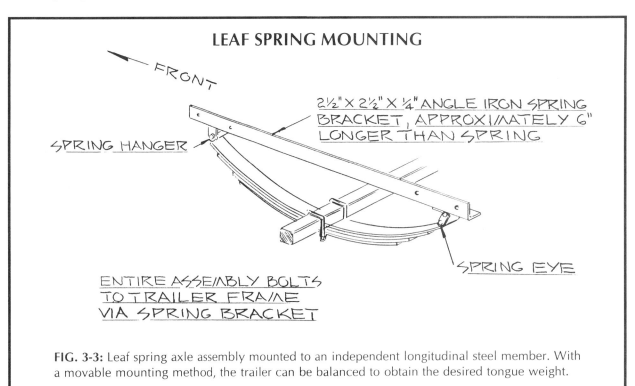

LEAF SPRING MOUNTING

FRONT

SPRING HANGER

2½" X 2½" X ¼" ANGLE IRON SPRING BRACKET, APPROXIMATELY 6" LONGER THAN SPRING

SPRING EYE

ENTIRE ASSEMBLY BOLTS TO TRAILER FRAME VIA SPRING BRACKET

FIG. 3-3: Leaf spring axle assembly mounted to an independent longitudinal steel member. With a movable mounting method, the trailer can be balanced to obtain the desired tongue weight.

CROSS TYPE LEAF SPRING

FIG. 3-5: A single cross leaf spring is acceptable for lightweight boats, but, without shock absorbers at each spring eye connecting to the trailer frame, the load tends to oscillate.

angle members that are in turn mounted to the trailer frame. Usually 1/4" by 2" x 2" or heavier steel angle is used to accommodate the spring eye and hanger. An undercarriage mounted on a movable platform, such as described, makes last minute adjustment simple for the best balance and tongue weight for the fully loaded boat trailer. The steel angle is bolted to the trailer frame with at least four 3/8" bolts with nuts and lock washers, or self-locking nuts. Fenders may be attached directly to the steel angle that supports the leaf spring. The length

of the steel angle member may be increased and step treads incorporated as shown in the "Fenders" section of Chapter 7.

It is essential that leaf springs be properly maintained. The shackle should be kept well greased and, after submersion, the springs should be washed off and sprayed with a leaf spring oil to prevent the internal layers from rusting. This is especially true when the trailer has been submerged in salt water. ❖

WHEELS, HUBS, AND TIRES

Chapter **4**

WHEELS

Trailer wheels come in various sizes and types. Automobile wheels can be used, either new or used, provided they can utilize a tire of adequate capacity for the load to be carried. New trailer wheels, however, are very inexpensive and often more cost effective to use than searching wrecking yards for automotive wheels in good shape. Trailer wheels are commonly available in diameters of 8", 9", 10", 12", 13", 14", 15", and 16". Wheels under 12" in diameter are usually confined to lightweight trailers.

Wheels come in a variety of configurations. Some small wheels split in two halves to put on the tire; larger wheels are available as drop center or semi-drop center types. (See FIG. 4-1.) The drop center wheel is used on automobiles and smaller trucks. The semi-drop center wheels are used on larger vehicles, will carry more weight, and utilize a tire and tube. Wheels also have varying amounts of "dish". Dish is the amount of offset from the hub bolting plate to the center of the wheel or tread of the tire. All of these factors must be considered when matching the wheel to the hub and trailer.

Overloaded wheels can crack and come apart with possible tragic results. A typical automobile wheel carries a load of one quarter of the gross vehicle weight on each wheel; or 1100 lbs. for a 4400 lb. car. Using two of these would give a capacity of 2200 lbs. for a standard single axle trailer. Be sure the wheels used are of an adequate capacity to carry the load.

The rims of the wheels selected should be undented and match identically. Dented rims prevent the tire bead from seating and is a frequent cause of blowouts. The typical new wheel will rust after several immersions, particularly in salt water so it is good practice to wire brush rims prior to installing the tire and give them a good coat of rust resisting paint.

The smaller the wheel, the closer the trailer will be to the ground. The boat may also extend over the top of the smaller wheels, eliminating the necessity of longer axles and their accompanying costs. The legal amount that the boat can extend past the tire, however, may be limited by state law. The greatest disadvantage of a small wheeled trailer is the number of revolutions the tires make in comparison to larger types to travel a given distance. Take the example of an 8" wheel that will have a tire diameter of about 18". At 50 MPH, this wheel will be rotating approximately 935 times each minute. On the other hand, a 15" wheel with tire diameter of about 30" would rotate approximately 560 times per minute at the same speed. The added rotation of small tires causes excessive bearing and tire wear along with heat buildup. Small wheels are best used when the load carried is light, the distance to be covered

20

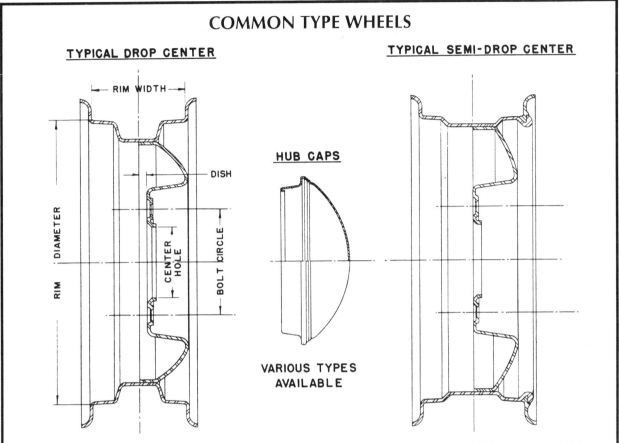

COMMON TYPE WHEELS

TYPICAL DROP CENTER

TYPICAL SEMI-DROP CENTER

RIM WIDTH

DISH

RIM DIAMETER

CENTER HOLE

BOLT CIRCLE

HUB CAPS

VARIOUS TYPES AVAILABLE

FIG. 4-1: (Left) Drop center wheel commonly used on trailers, automobiles, and light trucks. (Right) A semi-drop center wheel uses a tire and tube and is intended for heavier loads than the one at left.

is short, and slower speeds. Larger diameter wheels are always preferable for cross-country trailering, long trips, or heavy usage.

HUBS

The hub of the trailer is multipurpose; it must contain the bearings that ride on the spindle, hold the wheel and the brake drum, when used. Smaller wheels are not always mounted on hubs; the bearings can be in raceways in the wheel that ride directly on the spindle. Just as

with the other components of an undercarriage, the hubs also vary in capacity and must be matched to the gross trailer and load weight. The standard manufactured hubs are available with bolt hole patterns to match various wheels. It has been common practice in the past to match the trailer wheel to that of the towing vehicle as long as they have adequate load carrying capacity. The bolt pattern, thus, would match that of the hubs on the towing vehicle and the spare tire of the towing vehicle could be used on the trailer. Unfortunately, most current autos do not have spares, and the tires are

21

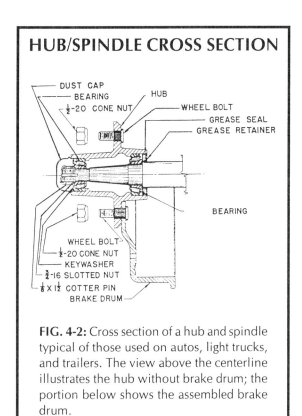

HUB/SPINDLE CROSS SECTION

DUST CAP
BEARING
½-20 CONE NUT
HUB
WHEEL BOLT
GREASE SEAL
GREASE RETAINER

BEARING

WHEEL BOLT
½-20 CONE NUT
KEYWASHER
¾-16 SLOTTED NUT
⅛ X 1½ COTTER PIN
BRAKE DRUM

FIG. 4-2: Cross section of a hub and spindle typical of those used on autos, light trucks, and trailers. The view above the centerline illustrates the hub without brake drum; the portion below shows the assembled brake drum.

of a radial type not intended for trailers; tires will be discussed further along in this Chapter.

MATCHING WHEELS TO HUBS

The diameter, bolt pattern, and lug or bolt type of the wheel and hub must match. The wheel should be placed on the hub and each bolt or nut hand tightened; don't wrench tighten them initially. Tighten one firmly, then go approximately opposite and tighten another; work around the hub alternating the pattern to snug the bolts or nuts into the wheel socket. Final tightening should cinch the wheels securely to the hub. If a torque wrench is available, tighten 1/2" diameter studs to 70-90 foot-pounds of torque, 9/16" from 110 to 140, and 5/8" from 125-140.

TIRES

In days gone by, any tire was a trailer tire. To-day there are passenger car tires essentially made to provide a good ride, light truck tires for heavier loads, and trailer tires. Trailer tires are generally designed with more durability, muscle, and bruise and impact resistance than the typical passenger car tire and carry an "ST" (special trailer) designation on the sidewall.

All tires have a group of numbers embossed on the sidewalls. The load range is a measure of tire carcass strength or "ply rating". Load range "A" is equivalent to a two-ply rating, "B" to a four-ply rating, "C" to a six-ply, and "D" to an eight-ply. Ratings go up to an "N" equivalent to a twenty-four-ply rating, but trailer tires are usually in the "B", "C", or "D" group. The drawings in FIG. 4-4 indicate the standard labeling method used to designate tire dimensions.

Trailer tires have taller sidewalls that flex more to cushion the ride; this is important, as most trailers do not have suspension systems and shock absorbers to help cushion road shock impacts. "ST" tires specifically designed for trailer use combine these features. Most new automobile tires are steel belted radial type; trailer tires are available with different configurations, bias-ply, bias-belted, and radial. See FIG. 4-3.

Bias-ply tires have the same number of plies on the sidewalls as on the tread. These are much like those used on our yesteryear automobiles. The side walls flex very little, but do provide a soft ride. Such tires do not always hold the tread to the pavement, and the rolling resistance is relatively high.

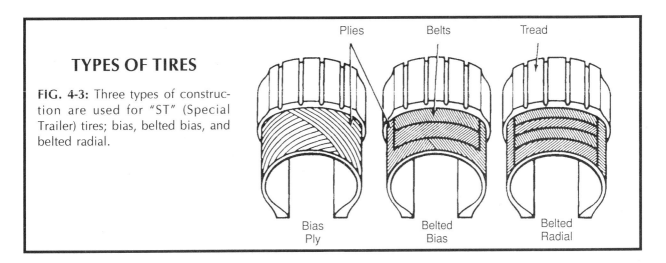

TYPES OF TIRES

FIG. 4-3: Three types of construction are used for "ST" (Special Trailer) tires; bias, belted bias, and belted radial.

Plies   Belts   Tread

Bias Ply   Belted Bias   Belted Radial

Bias-belted tires are a cross between bias-ply and radial construction, a bias-ply with belts under the ply. The rolling resistance of such a tire is slightly less than a bias-ply type and has greater traction and tread life.

Radial-ply tire plies run directly across the tire from bead to bead plus extra belts or plies (often of steel wire) under the tread encircling the perimeter. This enables the sidewalls to flex and have more of the tread on the pavement when cornering. Radial tires have longer life and improve fuel economy. However, passenger vehicle tires (designated "P" on the sidewall) are not the best choice for trailers. They may accentuate the tendency of a trailer to wander from side to side, and with their thin sidewalls, are more prone to punctures and ruptures. Also, passenger tires used in trailer applications must have their load capacities downgraded (multiply the passenger tire load capacity by .91 to determine the capacity for trailer application). To avoid the problems associated with passenger car tires use radial-ply tires intended especially for trailers with the "ST" designation.

But what happens if you use passenger car or light truck tires on a trailer? The ride will be rougher and the boat will have more of a tendency to bounce on the trailer; important considerations for any long distance trip.

The total weight carried (boat, motor, gear, and trailer divided by the number of tires) will give the required capacity for each tire. The maximum load on the tires should not exceed that stamped on their sidewall. However, tires of greater capacity are not considered detrimental. Inflate the tires to the pressure indicated on the sidewall. Over inflation may cause a blow-out in hot weather, and under inflation causes excessive trailer drag and wear on the tires. When shopping for "ST" tires there will be quite a variation in price. The load range of a tire is printed on the sidewall, and the higher the load rating the more the price. Trailer tires on sale usually have lower ratings, so be sure the tire you purchase has the desired load rating.

If the trailer is to be unused for a while, it is best to jack the trailer so the tires are not in contact with the ground or carrying any weight. If the trailer is left outdoors, cover the trailer

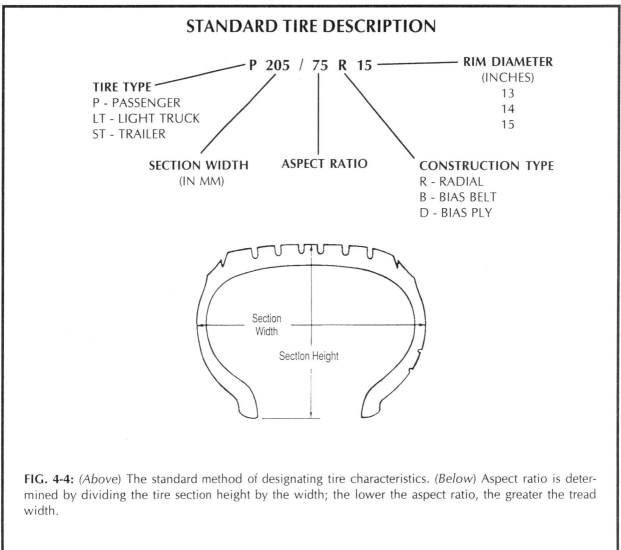

STANDARD TIRE DESCRIPTION

P 205 / 75 R 15

RIM DIAMETER
(INCHES)
13
14
15

TIRE TYPE
P - PASSENGER
LT - LIGHT TRUCK
ST - TRAILER

SECTION WIDTH
(IN MM)

ASPECT RATIO

CONSTRUCTION TYPE
R - RADIAL
B - BIAS BELT
D - BIAS PLY

Section Width

Section Height

FIG. 4-4: *(Above)* The standard method of designating tire characteristics. *(Below)* Aspect ratio is determined by dividing the tire section height by the width; the lower the aspect ratio, the greater the tread width.

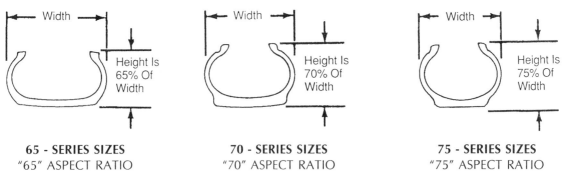

Width

Height Is 65% Of Width

Width

Height Is 70% Of Width

Width

Height Is 75% Of Width

65 - SERIES SIZES
"65" ASPECT RATIO

70 - SERIES SIZES
"70" ASPECT RATIO

75 - SERIES SIZES
"75" ASPECT RATIO

tires to protect them from the elements. With the limited use the ordinary boat trailer gets, probably more trailer tires wear out from rot or old age than tread wear. Check tires frequently for bad cracks or other signs of deterioration. All new passenger and trailer tires are date coded. The date is indicated following "DOT" embossed on the sidewall. The last three numbers following DOT indicate the month followed by the year. E.g. The numbers 026 would indicate that the tire was made in February of 1996.

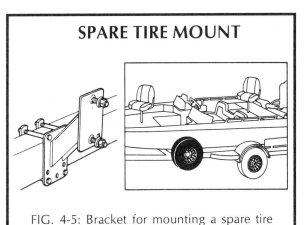

SPARE TIRE MOUNT

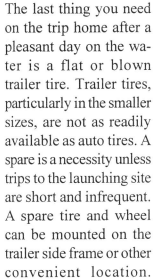

FIG. 4-5: Bracket for mounting a spare tire and wheel to the side of the trailer frame.

SPARE TIRE

The last thing you need on the trip home after a pleasant day on the water is a flat or blown trailer tire. Trailer tires, particularly in the smaller sizes, are not as readily available as auto tires. A spare is a necessity unless trips to the launching site are short and infrequent. A spare tire and wheel can be mounted on the trailer side frame or other convenient location. Trailer spares are also a frequent target of thieves, so lock your spare and trailer wheels securely. ❖

WHEEL BEARINGS

Wheel bearings slip over the axle spindle and support the hub that in turn carries the wheel and tire. The cavity between the hub and spindle is filled with grease to lubricate the bearings. The grease is kept in the spindle/hub cavity by seals and an outer cap. Most wheel bearings today are a tapered type with a greater load carrying capacity than the common roller bearing. It's a proven system, common to automobiles and most vehicles on the road.

It is seldom that one hears of wheel bearing failures on an automobile. Wheel bearing failure on boat trailers, however, is unfortunately quite common. Without warning a defective bearing can fail while towing the trailer down the highway. The result is most often freezing of the bearings causing failure of the wheel to rotate, and very possibly snapping of the axle spindle. Boat trailer wheels and hubs are most often partially submerged during launching or retrieving the boat, and the boat trailer bearings fail because water gets into the races and causes corrosion.

After the boat is trailed to the launching site, the hubs are hot. When the wheels are submerged during launching, the hubs suddenly cool and air inside unprotected hubs forms a vacuum that draws water and grit into the hubs and causes pitting of the bearings. The rough or pitted bearings create tremendous heat, much greater than the bearing grease will stand,

and may actually melt from the heat generated and fuse to the axle. Special bearing greases intended for boat trailers have a rust inhibitor but, unfortunately, do not eliminate the problem. The best way to prevent bearing failure on the boat trailer is to never submerge the wheel bearings in water. Unfortunately, this is often impractical or impossible. If, after being submerged, the bearings are removed, cleaned, and re-packed, the bearing failure problem will be eliminated. Most people, however, fail to take such precautions, and it is admittedly a task that is easy to overlook and not one most people will wish to do after a day on the water.

BEARING PROTECTOR DEVICES

Several bearing protector devices are made to combat bearing failure. Their purpose is to keep water out of the bearing and they do a good job. Any trailer that is submerged to any extent when launching should be equipped with bearing protectors. The widely used BEARING BUDDY has been around for a long time. This unit replaces the dust cover in the axle hub. The hub is filled with grease through a spring loaded piston that holds a slight constant pressure inside the hub. This higher pressure together with the hub being full of grease, keeps out water when the trailer is submerged. Since the hub is full of grease, both bearings are assured of lubrication, and the rear seals

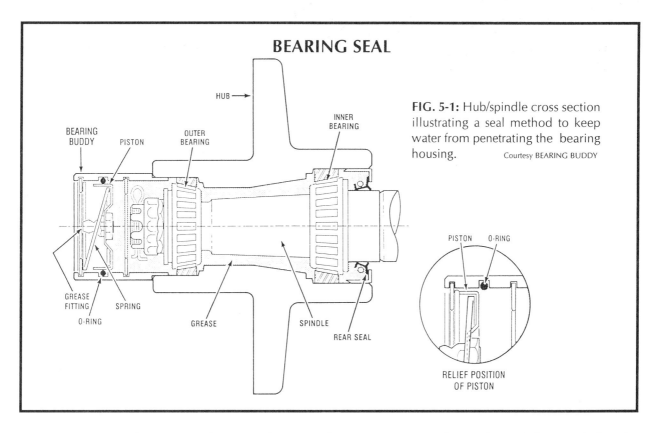

BEARING SEAL

FIG. 5-1: Hub/spindle cross section illustrating a seal method to keep water from penetrating the bearing housing. Courtesy BEARING BUDDY

last longer as they ride on a lubricated surface.

Other bearing protectors use similar methods to keep water from the bearings. The rear grease seal is a point of possible problems due to the pressure maintained in the hubs. Heavier duty seals either as standard or options help prevent failure.

WHEEL BEARING MAINTENANCE

Bearings must be kept clean; always keep the bearing cap intact. The bearings should be re-packed every two thousand miles or at least every season. In packing wheel bearings, the grease should be forced into the bearing races. If re-packing, wash off the bearing with kero-sene or gasoline and carefully check for pitting. If the bearings are pitted or discolored, they should be replaced. Those who trail their boats for long distances should carry grease and extra bearings with them at all times. After carefully fitting the grease retainers and bearings on the spindle, the adjusting nut is tightened with a wrench. At the same time, the wheel is turned in both directions until it will no longer turn freely to be sure that all the bearing surfaces contact. Back off the adjusting nut about a 1/4 turn to the nearest locking hold, or sufficiently to allow the wheel to rotate freely within the limits of .001" to .010" end play. Lock the nut in position with a cotter key or the locking device. ❖

BRAKES

The National Marine Manufacturers Association (NMMA) recommends that brakes be used when the total gross load of the trailer, boat, and gear exceeds 1500 lbs. The requirements for brakes on trailers vary considerably from state to state. Regardless of the legal requirements, the individual owes it to himself, his family, and others on the road to have an adequate brake system on his rig. People who have towed trailers without brakes can often recall it nearly jackknifing when attempting to stop quickly due to a signal, car, or obstruction up front. They may also remember coming down a steep grade and having the brakes start to fade and perhaps give out completely, even though proper braking procedures were used. Without question, most trailers carrying boats of any but the smaller types require brakes for safety.

Trailer brakes alter the towing characteristics dramatically. When stopping suddenly, you can be sure that the rig will come to a halt smoothly and evenly, without the feeling that someone is trying to shove your car. Brake fade out is minimized as you are applying brakes to all the wheels of both the towing vehicle and the trailer.

Boat trailer brakes must operate automatically when the towing vehicle's brakes are applied, or when the trailer separates from the towing vehicle while underway. There are three types of trailer brakes; mechanical, hydraulic, and

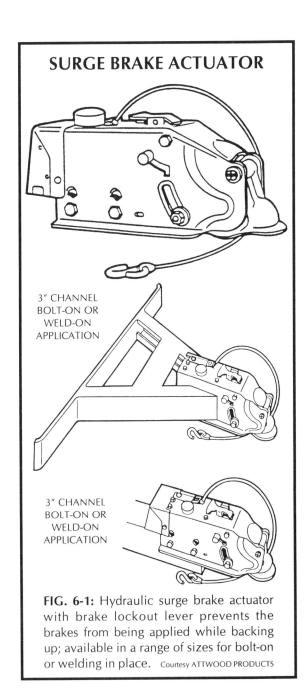

SURGE BRAKE ACTUATOR

3" CHANNEL BOLT-ON OR WELD-ON APPLICATION

3" CHANNEL BOLT-ON OR WELD-ON APPLICATION

FIG. 6-1: Hydraulic surge brake actuator with brake lockout lever prevents the brakes from being applied while backing up; available in a range of sizes for bolt-on or welding in place. Courtesy ATTWOOD PRODUCTS

TRAILER BRAKE RECOMMENDATIONS

TRAILER GROSS VEHICLE WEIGHT RATING (GVWR)	RECOMMENDED BRAKES
Up to 1500#	Brakes not required in most states. Check your state's laws and comply with tow vehicle manufacturer's requirements. One set of brakes may be helpful for loads over 1000#. One set of brakes should be considered.
1500# - 2500#	One set of brakes can help prevent sway and jackknifing that can occur during hard stops. Tow vehicles with unit body construction can flex if the trailer pushes hard against them during stopping and the resulting forces can transfer loads onto one or two wheels, giving uneven braking. Stopping capability is reduced and tire or vehicle damage can occur in a panic stop. Trailer brakes will help keep vehicles under control and reduce stopping distance.
2500# - 3500#	One set of brakes.
3000# - 4000#	One set of 10" brakes minimum. Two sets highly advisable, allowing shorter stopping distance and better control. Two sets of brakes can decrease trailer sway when braking from high speeds and reduce the potential for brake lockup (skidding) and brake overheating.
4000# - 7500#	Two sets of brakes on a tandom axle trailer. One set of 12" brakes (up to 5000#) on a single axle trailer.
7500# - 10,000#	Two sets of 12" brakes.
10,000# - 15,000#	Three sets of 12" brakes.

1. Safety considerations, especially emergency stopping capability, must be carefully considered when selecting brakes. Surviving one emergency situation without damage to trailer or tow vehicle or incurring personal injury is well worth the cost of brakes.

2. The tow vehicle and trailer combination should be capable of stopping in 200 feet (worst case), preferably less from the point at which brakes are applied from an initial speed of 55 m.p.h. (deceleration of 16ft./sec.). Shorter distances (150 ft. or less) are strongly recommended for safety.

3. Do not exceed tow vehicle manufacturer's maximum ratings for trailer towing, including Gross Combined Vehicle Weight Rating (GCWR).

4. A second set of brakes usually reduces stopping distance by about 50 feet at 55 m.p.h.

5. Consider towing conditions — heavy mountain travel, tow vehicle size in relation to load, etc.

6. Whenever the tow vehicle is lighter than the trailer, additional brakes are advisable.

7. Pickup trucks with light loads over the rear wheels are susceptible to jackknifing during panic stops if trailer brakes are inadequate.

FIG. 6-2: Recommendations given above are general guidelines as consideration must be given to the various trailer brake systems and tow vehicles.

electric. The mechanical type was used on older cars and is still common in other countries, although not in the US.

HYDRAULIC BRAKES

The hydraulic brake can be connected directly into the hydraulic brake system of the towing vehicle. The connection between the two systems plugs and unplugs readily with no loss of fluid or admittance of air. The hydraulic system does not use the fluid in the towing vehicle's braking system to actuate the trailer brakes directly. When the brakes of the towing vehicle are applied, the pressure operates what best can be called a slave cylinder, located on the trailer tongue, which in turn causes the trailer brakes to operate. Such a system synchronizes the car and trailer brakes. With most brake systems, the brakes can be set by tripping a lever on the tongue when the trailer is disconnected. This method does, however, involve some risk of disruption of the towing vehicles braking system. Due to higher cost and disapproval by auto manufacturers, hydraulic systems have not gained popularity.

ELECTRIC BRAKES

Most concur that electric brakes should not be used on a boat trailer that will have the wheels submerged during launching. The logical theory is that water and electricity is a poor mix and trouble will eventually occur. If the trailer will not be submerged, the possibilities of electric brake problems are virtually eliminated.

Electric brakes are activated through the towing vehicles electrical system and can be actuated by the foot pedal of the towing vehicle, or by a hand lever. These methods can be used singly or in combination. The foot pedal applies the brakes on the trailer and towing vehicle simultaneously. It is also possible to use a separate steering column lever to apply the trailer brakes alone. Obviously, it's poor practice to use the trailer brakes to slow the towing vehicle; a separate lever to actuate the trailer brakes, however, does provide advantages. If the trailer tends to sway or get out of hand on a rough or twisting road, a slight pressure of the trailer brakes will straighten it out immediately. Connection of the electric brake system to the towing vehicle is accomplished by using an electrical connector loom between the towing vehicle and the trailer system.

Breakaway systems are used to actuate the brakes should a separation from the towing vehicle occur. The typical breakaway system requires a battery on the trailer near the hitch, Connected to a switch that actuates the brakes through a lanyard connected to the towing vehicle. when the tow vehicle and trailer are separated, the lanyard actuates the brakes.

SURGE BRAKES

Surge brakes can be either electrically or hydraulically operated. A surge brake is motivated by the surge of inertia of the trailer. As the car slows, the trailer tongue moves forward applying pressure in direct proportion to the car braking. A shock absorber assures smooth, even application of the trailer brakes in the exact amount needed. With surge brakes, no special connection to the car is needed. The entire braking system is self-contained on the trailer. Thus, the trailer can be towed by more than one family vehicle without expensive wiring or hook up to the towing vehicle. At a constant forward speed, the system has no pressure on the trailer wheel brake cylinders. To back up, some units require a special solenoid switch or a manually operated block out pin. Without some type of protection when backing up, particularly up a hill, the surge would be forward, tending to lock the brakes. One company uses a self-energizing hydraulic brake system that produces maximum brake output when stopping, yet will permit easy back up. When backing up on level ground, there is no braking. When backing up a hill or over an obstacle, there is braking; but since the brakes are not self-energizing when backing up, braking output is only 10% of what it would be with the trailer moving forward. This slight amount of braking during back up can be easily overcome by the vehicle.

Weight distributing hitches help provide a level ride and may improve braking; if such a hitch is used, make sure it does not interfere with proper actuator operation. The actuator must compress to energize brakes and fully extend to release them. See Chapter 10 for more details on weight distributing hitches.

A breakaway mechanism that actuates trailer brakes should it become disconnected from the towing vehicle, is also used on surge brake systems. No one expects a trailer to become disconnected while being towed, but a breakaway is insurance should such an occurrence take place.

MAINTENANCE

Any braking system on a boat trailer increases maintenance problems, especially when the wheels and brakes are often submerged. Water in the brake drum mechanism can cause corrosion and the resultant problems. Constant maintenance and inspection are an absolute necessity. Consideration should also be given to the fact that trailer brakes that have been submerged will not operate efficiently until dried out. This is similar to the problem occurring on an automobile when going through deep puddles of water. Use the same precautions; put pressure on the brakes to dry out the bands. ❖

TRAILER FRAMES

Trailer frames may be constructed from steel shapes such as angle, channel, pipe, and tubing (round, square or rectangular). It is also possible to use wood for trailer frames, although such usage is not commonplace. Aluminum trailers, although light in weight, are expensive to fabricate. From a simplicity standpoint, most trailer frames are made from steel shapes.

Standard structural steel angle sections can be used for smaller trailer frames with under 700 lbs. maximum capacity. Such lightweight trailer frames are usually vee shaped (commonly called "A" frame) with bunks or cradles fastened directly to angle iron longitudinals. Tubing or pipe can also be used for such frames; or combinations of steel tubing, angle or other sections.

Both square and rectangular tubing for trailer frames have advantages and disadvantages. Tubing is lightweight with high strength, however, tubing is difficult to seal completely, and water will often get into the tubular portion during launching. This, of course, will promote corrosion problems over a period of time. Trailers built from tubular sections, however, are neater in appearance and are favored by the individual who wants the sharpest and cleanest rig. Most small or medium sized boat trailer frames are built from rectangular or square tubing.

Pipe or round tubing has the same qualifica-

tions as rectangular tubing for trailer frames, but is very difficult to fit together and weld at junctions. Galvanized pipe can be obtained relatively inexpensively, and may seem an ideal solution to the rust problem inherent in boat trailer frames. However, welding galvanized material can be dangerous due to the great amount of zinc fumes that are released. Then too, galvanized material is broken down by the heat of the welding and cutting, and the integrity of the weld may be questionable. The longitudinal bending strength of pipe is such that a trailer built with it is usually only used for loads totaling less than 700 lbs., unless supported by a truss arrangement.

Specially shapes of steel can be used in trailer frame fabrication. The 18' trailer shown in FIG. 7-1 is constructed from 10 gage steel formed in the shape of a channel member with a 2" flange and 4" upright web.

Steel channel is readily available and is easy to fabricate into a viable trailer frame. The heights of the upright portion, web thickness, and flange widths are obtainable in varying sizes to fit most applications. Junctions of typical trailer frame members built from steel channel are illustrated in FIG. 7-2.

FIG. 7-2A illustrates a common method of joining cross members to longitudinals. The flanges are cut away to make a tongue that fits into the open side of the channel mem-

TRAILERS FOR INBOARD BOATS

FIG. 7-1: Tandem axle "A" frame type trailers for a typical inboard boat with vee drive or centrally located motor. All frame members are 10 gage steel formed into channel sections.

ber; after welding all around, a very strong junction results. Welding the members as shown in FIG. 7-2E is poor practice and could fracture under stress.

FIG. 7-2B illustrates an excellent cross member type of fabrication when the web portion of the channel is faced inward. This does leave something to be desired in appearance, and causes difficulty in anchoring the angle member that secures the spring (Chapter 3, FIG. 3-3). With proper location of the cross members, however, the upright flange of the angle can be turned inward.

FIG. 7-2C and 7-2D are quite strong and have the advantage of enabling the centerline of the boat or keel to be dropped lower than the longitudinals, and is especially adaptable to hulls that have considerable vee in the bottom

or sailboats with swing or small fixed keels.

The cross member method shown in FIG. 7-2F junctions with the side rail member, as shown in FIG. 7-2A or 7-2B. The center of the cross member drops down in a vee — another method of dropping the keel below the longitudinals.

The greater the overall trailer length, the more the bending stresses on the frame. One solution is to use larger longitudinal members, however, this increases the weight and also the cost of the materials. A truss, as illustrated in FIG. 7-3, will add considerable strength, enable the trailer to be made longer without the danger of deflection, and yet retain lightweight construction. Although this truss is illustrated as being fabricated from pipe or rod, flat stock, usually 3/16" to 1/4" in thickness and 1" to 1 1/4" wide can be substituted.

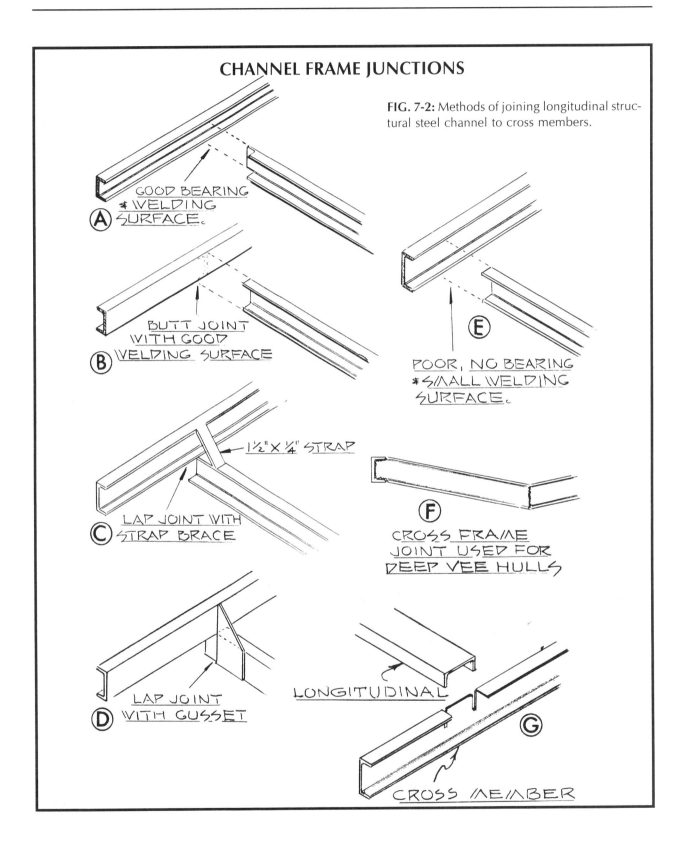

CHANNEL FRAME JUNCTIONS

FIG. 7-2: Methods of joining longitudinal structural steel channel to cross members.

(A) GOOD BEARING & WELDING SURFACE.

(B) BUTT JOINT WITH GOOD WELDING SURFACE

(C) LAP JOINT WITH STRAP BRACE — 1½" X ¼" STRAP

(D) LAP JOINT WITH GUSSET

(E) POOR, NO BEARING & SMALL WELDING SURFACE.

(F) CROSS FRAME JOINT USED FOR DEEP VEE HULLS

(G) LONGITUDINAL — CROSS MEMBER

WOODEN FRAMES

Wooden trailer frames are not common, but are practical if properly constructed. A wooden trailer will float; and some consider this a definite advantage in launching and retrieving the boat. Securing cross members to the longitudinals and attaching the undercarriage is a major problem with wooden trailers. Commonly, steel clips are used at the junctions of the cross members, and the longitudinals are through bolted into each member. Longitudinals will seldom be less than 2" x 6" for even the smaller trailers. The type of wood used may vary, however, any material should be first quality and free from shakes or knots that would tend to weaken the strength of the member. FIG. 7-5 illustrates a trailer with 3" x 8" clear fir longitudinal members made to carry an 18' cabin cruiser with a total weight of about 2800 lbs.

INBOARD FRAMES

Boats powered with in-line or vee drive inboard engines have underwater gear, strut, rudder, propeller, and shaft that must be protected when trailering or launching. These appendages project below the bottom of the boat and a cage or cutaway of the centerline framework is necessary. The standard

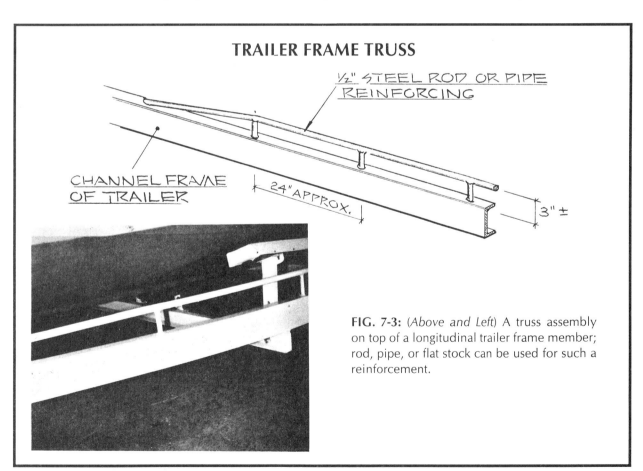

TRAILER FRAME TRUSS

½" STEEL ROD OR PIPE REINFORCING

CHANNEL FRAME OF TRAILER

24" APPROX.

3" ±

FIG. 7-3: (*Above and Left*) A truss assembly on top of a longitudinal trailer frame member; rod, pipe, or flat stock can be used for such a reinforcement.

how to build boat trailers

"GLEN-L #2100 SERIES" TRAILER

FIG. 7-4: GLEN-L Series # 2100 trailer frame constructed from 4" steel channel to accommodate an 18' 6" inboard runabout. **2** and **3**: The flanges of the cross channel are cut away to fit into the longitudinal member. **4**: The central area is dropped down in the aft section to accommodate the rudder, strut, and propeller appendages. **5**: The spring/axle assembly welded to a longitudinal angle is temporarily clamped in place, but will later be bolted in place at the correct position to obtain the desired balance. **6**: The coupler has a 50° angle to cap the ends of the longitudinals.

WOODEN TRAILER FRAME

FIG. 7-5: Trailer frame built from 3" x 8" lumber to accommodate an 18', 2800 lb. boat. The longitudinal side members were slit vertically (kerfed) and re-glued together after bending to shape. Trailer frames for heavier boats were reinforced with a 1" x 8" lamination glued to the longitudinal member. Cross members and forms are limited, but these trailers have had extensive use without problems.

how to build boat trailers

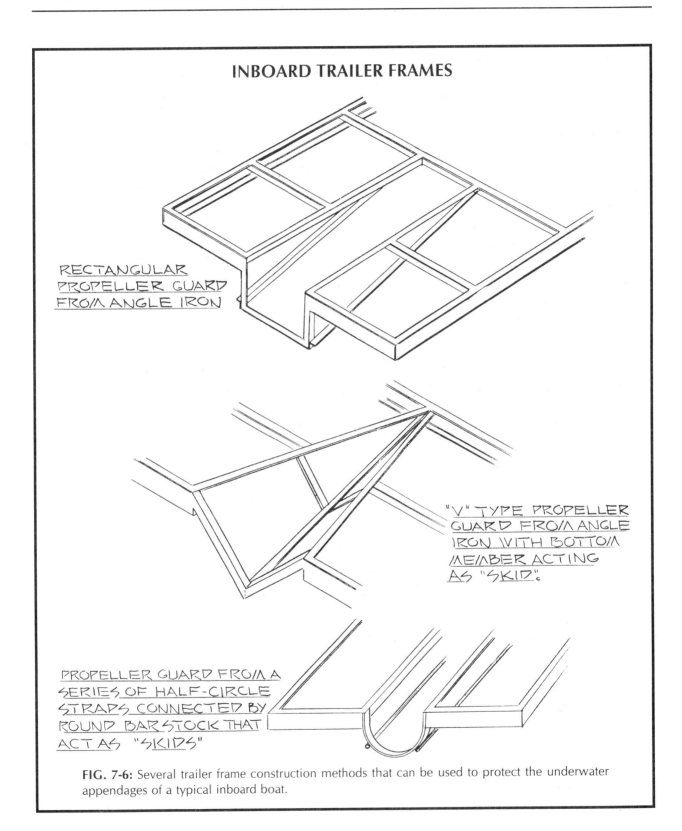

INBOARD TRAILER FRAMES

RECTANGULAR PROPELLER GUARD FROM ANGLE IRON

"V" TYPE PROPELLER GUARD FROM ANGLE IRON WITH BOTTOM MEMBER ACTING AS "SKID".

PROPELLER GUARD FROM A SERIES OF HALF-CIRCLE STRAPS CONNECTED BY ROUND BAR STOCK THAT ACT AS "SKIDS"

FIG. 7-6: Several trailer frame construction methods that can be used to protect the underwater appendages of a typical inboard boat.

method is to cut away all cross members in the center area from about the midpoint of the trailer aft. Longitudinals connect these members and frequent "U", "V", or rectangular cutouts are used, as shown in FIG. 7-6. Cross members are very important, as they keep the side longitudinals that the spring assembly is mounted to, from twisting. If these cross members are made undersize or are too few in number, excessive racking of the trailer frame may take place. It is desirable to have a longitudinal member running from the lowest point of the aft cutout forward to the trailer chassis, acting like a skid to prevent hooking the lowered trailer cross member when running down a drive or going over a bump.

Many shapes of trailer frames can be used, as shown by the numerous photos and drawings that accompany this chapter. One important point should be considered whenever possible; the side longitudinals should extend in one piece as far forward and aft as practical, or sufficient laps of longitudinal members should be made to provide a rigid structure. It is also advisable to make the bend as close to the forward point of the spring shackle as possible.

FRAME ALIGNMENT

It is imperative that the trailer chassis tongue or coupler be in the exact center of the trailer, and the axle placed at right angles to the centerline. If the wheels are out of alignment or the trailer hitch off center, the trailer may well track to one side, and excessive tire

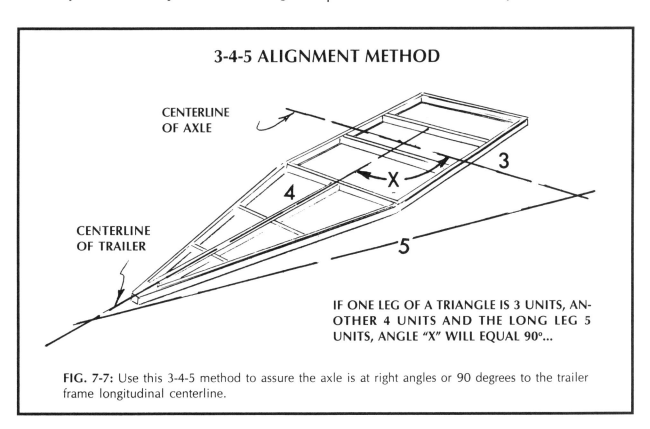

3-4-5 ALIGNMENT METHOD

CENTERLINE OF AXLE

CENTERLINE OF TRAILER

3

4

X

5

IF ONE LEG OF A TRIANGLE IS 3 UNITS, ANOTHER 4 UNITS AND THE LONG LEG 5 UNITS, ANGLE "X" WILL EQUAL 90°...

FIG. 7-7: Use this 3-4-5 method to assure the axle is at right angles or 90 degrees to the trailer frame longitudinal centerline.

TILTING TRAILER FORM

FIG. 7-8: This longitudinal trailer form, primarily used for smaller lightweight boats, tilts so the boat can be launched or retrieved easily. Rollers on the tilting bed would make rolling the boat off easier.

wear may occur. A simple method for aligning the axle at right angles to the centerline is the "3-4-5" method illustrated in FIG. 7-7.

TILT TRAILERS

A tilt trailer is one that hinges from the tongue while still connected to the towing vehicle. The boat can thus be slid from the trailer into the water, and retrieved with a winch on the trailer tongue quite easily. If the launching area is paved or hard packed and the rig is able to be backed to the water's edge, or if the launching ramp is steep enough to launch the boat without getting the wheel bearings wet, then a tilt-bed should be given serious consideration. Obviously a tilt bed trailer is not for heavier boats with inboards or keeled sailboats. On the other hand, if the areas you launch in are more

diverse and conditions not always ideal, the tilt-bed may not be needed.

A tilt-bed trailer is more difficult and expensive to build and creates structural and maintenance problems. These are surmountable conditions, however. The more common tilt trailer for smaller boats is actually a tilt-bed or form, as shown in FIG. 7-8. This type of tilting bed does not have many of the problems that the fully pivoting trailer frame causes. It can be built on any conventional flat trailer.

The true tilt trailer breaks on a pivot or hinge to allow the aft portion of the trailer frame to tilt from the tongue. Many different devices are used to provide a solid pivot and a positive locking mechanism when the tilt is not being used. FIG. 7-9 illustrates a pivot that is fastened to a cross member of the trailer frame. The trailer tongue pivots about this junction by the use of a bolt through hinge ears and the trailer tongue. When the tongue is held in the non-use position, it rests securely in a close-fitting inverted "U" bracket. The tongue is held to the frame by a rod or bolt through the tongue and the angled section of the "U" bracket. Other methods use a bolt or rod extending through the longitudinal trailer frame and the tongue. The two points that are critical are the pivot and the point of connection between the tongue and the trailer. Movement at either of these points could create future problems.

A tilt mechanism for larger trailers is shown in the photographs, and the drawings in FIG. 7-10 and 7-11. This type of tilt arrangement can be adapted to almost any "A" frame type of trailer. It is very strong, as the strain is all on the trailer hitch, and, when used in combination with a jack lift stand to mechanically lift

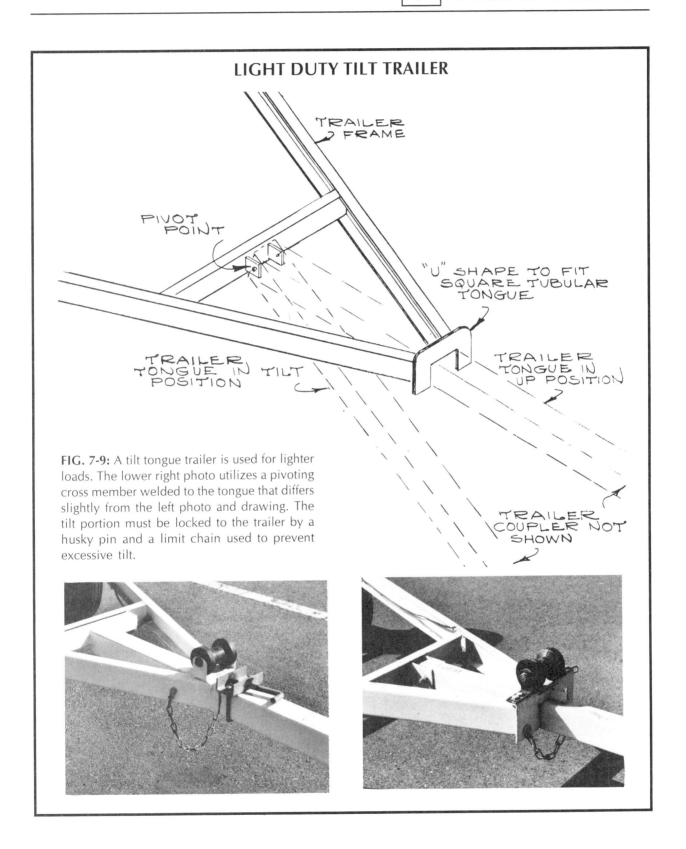

LIGHT DUTY TILT TRAILER

TRAILER FRAME

PIVOT POINT

"U" SHAPE TO FIT SQUARE TUBULAR TONGUE

TRAILER TONGUE IN TILT POSITION

TRAILER TONGUE IN UP POSITION

TRAILER COUPLER NOT SHOWN

FIG. 7-9: A tilt tongue trailer is used for lighter loads. The lower right photo utilizes a pivoting cross member welded to the tongue that differs slightly from the left photo and drawing. The tilt portion must be locked to the trailer by a husky pin and a limit chain used to prevent excessive tilt.

how to build boat trailers

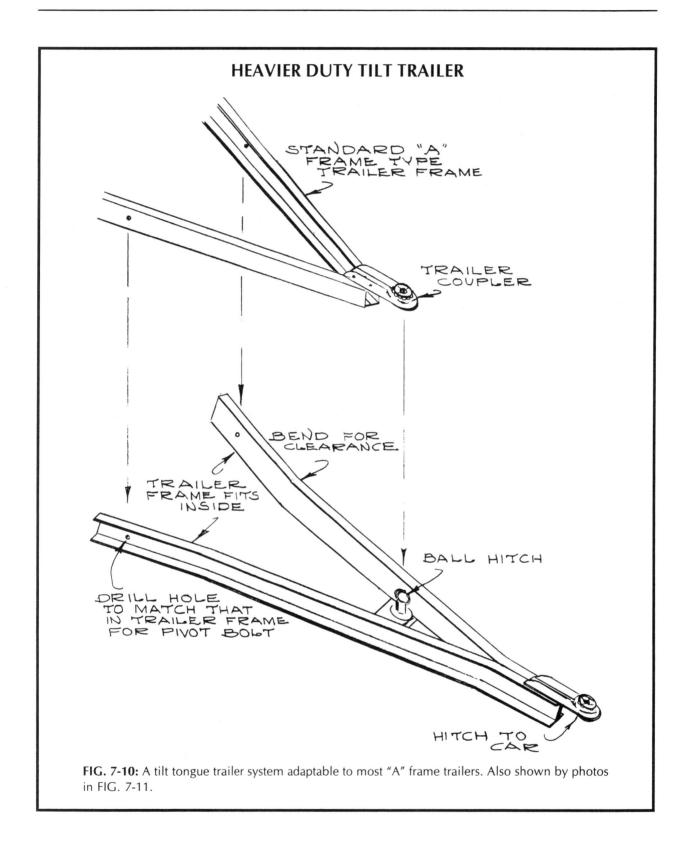

HEAVIER DUTY TILT TRAILER

STANDARD "A" FRAME TYPE TRAILER FRAME

TRAILER COUPLER

BEND FOR CLEARANCE

TRAILER FRAME FITS INSIDE

BALL HITCH

DRILL HOLE TO MATCH THAT IN TRAILER FRAME FOR PIVOT BOLT

HITCH TO CAR

FIG. 7-10: A tilt tongue trailer system adaptable to most "A" frame trailers. Also shown by photos in FIG. 7-11.

HEAVIER DUTY TILT TRAILER

FIG. 7-11: The tilt tongue of this trailer is shown in the traveling position above. *(Below)* The trailer is shown tilted by a screw jack to adjust and limit the degree of tilt.

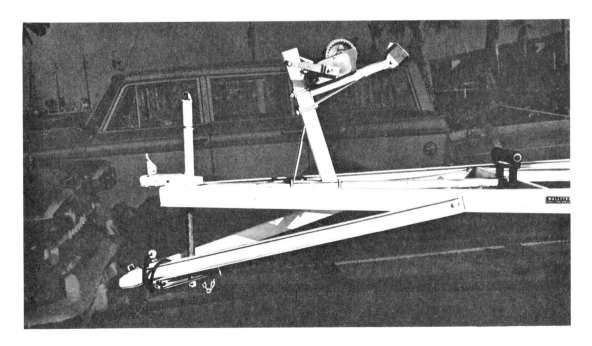

how to build boat trailers

TRAILER FRAMES

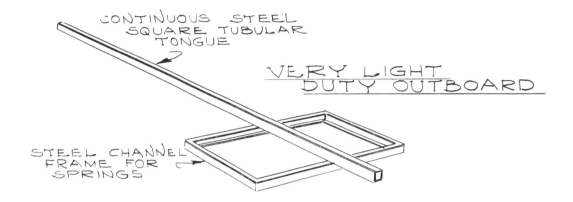

FIG. 7-12A: Lightweight trailer frame that can be built from various structural steel shapes. The frame shown uses square tubing for the tongue and channel for the frame.

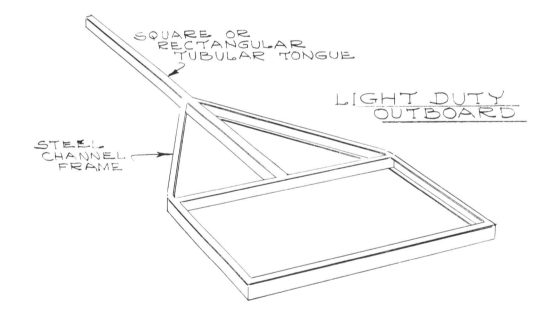

FIG. 7-12B: The load capacity of this trailer frame can vary considerably depending on the sizes of structural steel used.

and control the tilt of the trailer bed, launching and retrieving is greatly simplified. The mechanical lift tilt-bed trailer makes it possible to handle larger and heavier boats without undue effort.

Tilt trailers designed to carry all but the smallest boats should have a device limiting the amount of the tilt. This can be in the form of a safety chain or a controlled jack lift.

POINTS TO CONSIDER

The length of a trailer should be as long as the boat plus tongue clearance, however, the position of the trailer hitch and type of towing vehicle will vary this distance. Consider a van or pickup truck with a hitch mounted close to the aft end of the vehicle. What happens if such a combination goes through a sharp dip or makes a sharp turn? The boat could easily contact the van or truck body and damage one or both. The higher the bow of the boat and the greater the bow beam (as with a catamaran), the more acute the problem becomes. Although it's good practice to keep the overall trailer length as short as possible, don't forget the clearance between the boat and towing vehicle.

A decision should be made as to whether the boat will be carried between the wheels of the trailer or over them. After the selection of the axle and undercarriage components, the trailer frame should be figured to be as wide as possible, and compatible with the maximum spring center widths of the axle being used. Trailer shapes vary considerably; the sketches illustrate a few of the more popular types. Larger trailers capable of carrying a greater load almost universally use the "A" type frame with

possible minor variations.

It is desirable, whenever possible, for the side members of an "A" frame or similar type to extend the full length of the trailer. An example of a continuous side frame member is shown in FIG. 7-4. Weld the cross members to the longitudinals aft of the point the framework will start to bend to the coupler. In most instances, steel channel longitudinals can be bent to the coupler without cutting and welding; welded longitudinals tend to promote twisting of the frame. A little muscle power with a come-along and possibly some heat at the bending point will usually enable the forward ends to be bent together. Hammering the longitudinal at the bending point will also help ease the bending stress.

The selection of the size and type of steel for the trailer requires numerous calculations of the stresses involved that are beyond most individuals and the scope of this text. In compiling sizes of structural members, many trailers were investigated to obtain a practical viewpoint of what size to use. The following information should suffice for almost all trailers operating under average conditions. The weights given are for the load to be carried; which includes the boat, motor, gear, plus the weight of the trailer.

The capacity of the trailer in FIG. 7-12A (top) would approximate 700 lbs. total with a length limit of 14'. This trailer utilizes a 2" x 1" x 3/16" steel channel frame with a 2 1/2" x 2 1/2" tubular square tongue that has a .125 wall thickness.

The trailer in FIG. 7-12B has the same maximum length, but with a capacity of 900 lbs., utilizes a 2 1/2" x 2 1/2" tubular square tongue that has a .125 wall thickness. The frame is 2"

how to build boat trailers

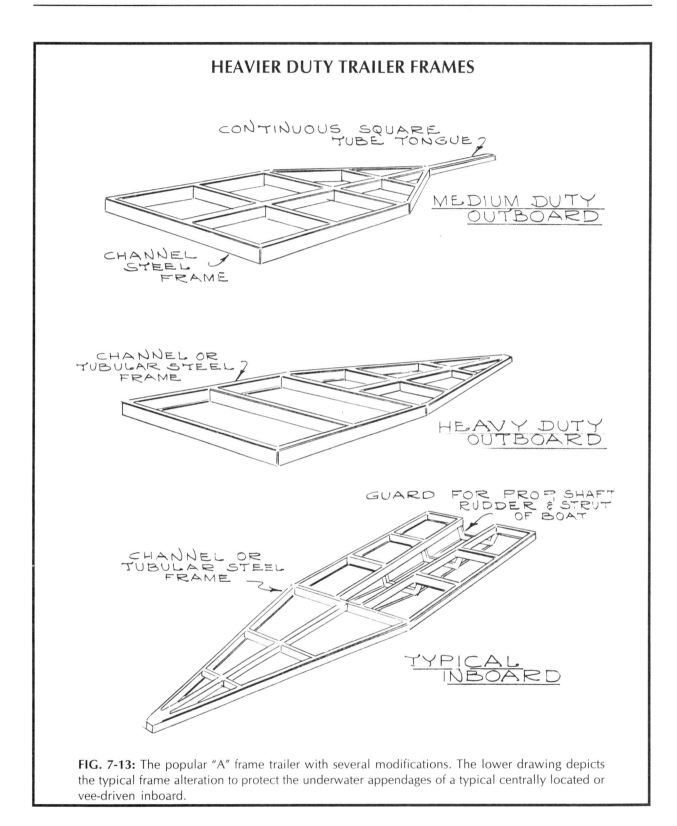

HEAVIER DUTY TRAILER FRAMES

CONTINUOUS SQUARE TUBE TONGUE

MEDIUM DUTY OUTBOARD

CHANNEL STEEL FRAME

CHANNEL OR TUBULAR STEEL FRAME

HEAVY DUTY OUTBOARD

GUARD FOR PROP SHAFT RUDDER & STRUT OF BOAT

CHANNEL OR TUBULAR STEEL FRAME

TYPICAL INBOARD

FIG. 7-13: The popular "A" frame trailer with several modifications. The lower drawing depicts the typical frame alteration to protect the underwater appendages of a typical centrally located or vee-driven inboard.

x 1" channel with a 3/16" web.

FIG. 7-13 depicts the popular "A" frame trailer that can be constructed for many different loads by varying the size of the structural members. "A" frame trailers, for the individual builder, are most easily fabricated from steel channel. Trailers with a maximum length of approximately 14' and with loads to 700 lbs. total will use 2" x 1" channel with a 3/16" web. Trailers with a maximum length of about 18' and loads to 2000 lbs. are usually built with 3", 4.10 lbs. per foot channel. Trailer lengths to 20' with loads to about 2600 lbs. require an additional truss, as shown in FIG. 7-3. Optionally 4", 5.40 lbs. per foot channel can be used without the truss in this size range; and the total load can be increased to 3500 lbs. Total loads to 5000 lbs. on trailers 25' long may use 4", 5.4 lb. channel with a truss, or a 5", 6.70 lbs. per foot channel without truss.

The total weight of the rig, including the boat, motor, and trailer, is imperative to properly determine the trailer required. The weight of the boat must include the fuel and all gear to be carried. Don't overlook the gear. Such gear would include anchors, line, groceries, camping equipment, folding seats — you name it. If it is to be carried in the boat, it is gear. Try not to guess; weigh the boat whenever possible. It will usually weigh more than your estimate. In addition to the boat, the various components that make up the trailer must be figured. The charts that follow provide weights of various sizes of steel members common to trailer frame construction. The weight per foot is given to enable the prospective builder to determine the total weight of steel in the trailer frame. Weights of the other components, undercarriage, jack stands, etc., can be obtained from the manufacturer's literature.

STEEL CHANNEL

Steel channel comes in many structural sizes but for trailers 3", 4" and 5" are most commonly used. This particular dimension refers to the overall height, however, other specifications are needed to completely describe the size. The common method of designating structural steel channel, in addition to the overall height, is by weight in pounds per lineal foot. Channel steel in the smaller sizes is designated by the height, width of the flange, and web thickness. Dimensions, weights, and sizes of typical steel channel are noted in the following charts:

STEEL CHANNEL- Hot Rolled

Dimensions, Inches	Web Inches	Approx. Wt- lbs. per lin. ft
2" x 1"	1/8"	1.78
2" x 1"	3/16"	2.57
2 1/2" x 5/8"	3/16"	2.27

STRUCTURAL SIZES
Spec. ASTM A7-521

Sizes Inches	Approx. Wt lbs. per ft.	Flange Width in inches	Web Thickness decimal of an inch
3"	4.10	1.410	.170
3"	5.00	1.498	.258
3"	6.00	1.596	.356
4"	5.40	1.580	.180
4"	6.25	1.647	.247
4"	7.25	1.720	.320
5"	6.70	1.750	.190
5"	9.00	1.855	.325
6"	8.20	1.920	.200
6"	10.50	2.034	.314

Other sizes omitted as they are not common to the usual boat trailer.

STEEL ANGLES

Steel angles ("L" shaped) are dimensioned by the lengths of the upright and base plus the

how to build boat trailers

web thickness. Typical sizes with their weights are listed in the following chart:

Dimensions, inches	Approx. Weight in lbs. per lin. ft.
2" x 2" x 1/8"	1.65
2" x 2" x 3/16"	2.44
2" x 2" x 1/4"	3.19
2" x 2" x 5/16"	3.92
2" x 2" x 3/8"	4.70
2 1/2" x 1 1/2" x 3/16"	2.44
2 1/2" x 1 1/2" x 1/4"	3.19
2 1/2" x 2" x 3/16"	2.75
2 1/2" x 2" x 1/4"	3.62

TUBULAR SQUARE SECTIONS

Square tubing is specified by outside wall thickness in either decimals of an inch or by the SAE standard "Birmingham Gage" method. Square tubing is available either seamless or with a welded joint. The latter is most often used in trailer frames.

Size in inches	Wall Thickness in decimals of an inch	Approx. wt. in lbs., per foot
2" x 2"	.065	1.711
2" x 2"	.095	2.461
2" x 2"	.125	3.187

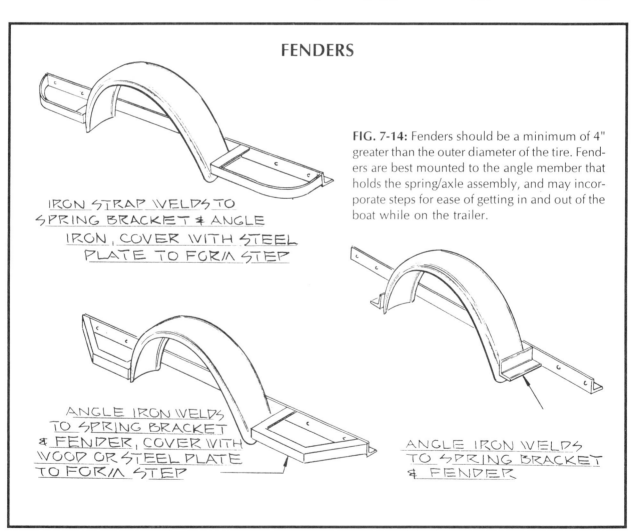

FENDERS

IRON STRAP WELDS TO SPRING BRACKET & ANGLE IRON, COVER WITH STEEL PLATE TO FORM STEP

ANGLE IRON WELDS TO SPRING BRACKET & FENDER, COVER WITH WOOD OR STEEL PLATE TO FORM STEP

FIG. 7-14: Fenders should be a minimum of 4" greater than the outer diameter of the tire. Fenders are best mounted to the angle member that holds the spring/axle assembly, and may incorporate steps for ease of getting in and out of the boat while on the trailer.

ANGLE IRON WELDS TO SPRING BRACKET & FENDER

FIG. 7-15A: (*Left*) Trailer built from 3/4" pipe with webs of flat metal. Trailer carries a 16' boat with a weight of approximately 1700 lbs. (*Right*) Small 14' trailer for outboard made from 2" pipe.

FIG. 7-15B: (*Left*) Trailer for a 24' boat with a weight of approximately 3800 lbs. Constructed from 4" longitudinal steel channel and truss with 3" channel cross members. (*Right*) Trailer for a 21' cabin cruiser weighing approximately 3200 lbs. Trailer construction is of 4" channel; note that the four longitudinal members extend full length.

FIG. 7-15C: (*Upper Left*) Trailer for a 17' boat with a weight of approximately 1700 lbs. Trailer is constructed from 10 gage 2"x4" tubular section. (*Left*) Trailer for a 13' sailboat of approximately 400 lbs. Trailer is constructed from 1"x2"x3/16" steel channel. (*Above*) A graphic illustration of a trailer constructed from 2" pipe that has been too heavily loaded. The long tongue would never support much weight.

2 1/2" x 2 1/2"	.065	2.152
2 1/2" x 2 1/2"	.125	4.038
2 1/2" x 2 1/2"	.180	5.679
3" x 3"	.125	4.888
3" x 3"	.180	6.903

FENDERS

Fenders are not required by law in most states but without them the side of that pretty boat will soon be a mess. Fenders deflect water, road dirt and debris thrown off the tires down and away from the boat. There are various sizes and types of fenders, but essentially their purpose is to cover the area above the tire and yet provide clearance required for the springs or torsion axle movements. If the clearance between tire and fender is inadequate and the trailer is driven over a pot hole, the tire-to-fender contact can raise havoc. FIG. 7-16 illustrates very poor positioning for a fender on a dual axle

FIG. 7-16: An example of lack of sufficient clearance between tire and fender; the sharp edge of the fender rim could hit the tire and cause serious damage.

system. The sharp lip of the fender could easily hit the tire, and the clearance to compensate for road shocks and axle swing is not adequate.

Several methods of mounting fenders to the trailer frame are shown in FIG. 7-14. A bracket from fender-to-frame to incorporate a step is advantageous especially for large wheeled trailers. An upright baffle to seal the inner fender from the trailer, although not shown, is desirable and when padded, acts as a guide and further protection for the boat sides.

LAYOUT AND WELDING

A properly executed weld can produce a bond that will be as strong as the material used. In practice, however, the strength of a weld can vary considerably, primarily with the skill of the welder and the equipment used. Junctions of steel trailers should be electric arc welded by a competent welder.

Prior to welding, the junctions of steel trailer frame members should be fitted as close as possible. Make a chalk drawn layout of the trailer frame on a concrete floor where the trailer is being built. Start by laying out a centerline with the cross members marked at right angles. Use the "3-4-5" method shown in FIG. 7-7 to assure that cross members are perpendicular to the centerline. Rectangular or square sections of the trailer frame can be checked for squareness by making diagonal dimensions equal.

Cut the steel to size, marking the lengths directly from the layout. A cut-off saw is ideal to make clean accurate cuts, however, with care, an acetylene torch can be used. Take care that all members are positioned correctly and the frame is aligned for squareness. Block the frame from the ground or floor so it is level, and clamp or hold the parts together while tack welding. After the framework is tack welded, recheck the dimensions and squareness of the assembled parts. When all is in alignment, use a penetration weld around each junction.

All slag should be removed from welded joints and the seams ground smooth. After welding, the trailer should be cleaned of all rust, oil, or dirt in preparation for painting. Drill any necessary holes for bolt on members or runs of wiring. With proper forethought repainting should not be necessary.

PAINTING

Best results are obtained by spraying on metal surfaces; brush marks are inevitable and corners difficult to coat with a brush. Use paint that is especially formulated for metal. Buy a good quality product and follow the manufacturer's recommendations. Start with a primer coat such as red oxide, zinc chromate, or similar product to provide better adherence to the steel and a base for the finish paint. Follow the primer with a tack coat of acrylic enamel, industrial enamel, or rust inhibiting paint. Allow this coat to set and repeat the process with another coat to improve the protecting ability of the paint. Be sure to get paint into corners. Take extra care on the underside of the frame. Roll the frame over if possible or raise it on sturdy supports so overhead spraying will be easier. ❖

COUPLERS

The coupler mounts on the trailer tongue and links the trailer to the towing vehicle. It must withstand forces of pushing, pulling, twisting, both forward and side to side. Essentially it is a universal joint that connects the towing vehicle to the trailer. Although there are numerous types of couplers, using lunettes, pintle hooks, clevises, etc., the most common type for boat trailers is the ball coupler.

The ball coupler consists of a ball and a coupler. Ball couplers can be obtained in various capacities with the ball sizes becoming larger as the capacity of the coupler increases. The coupler must match the ball size; consider the ball and coupler a matched set. Couplers are available that are adaptable to various types of trailer tongues, such as pipe, channel, and rectangular shapes. Most "A" frame and medium to heavy duty trailers use a coupler hitch that caps the forward end of the trailer frame; a 50 degree angularity is somewhat standard. Capping couplers can be obtained with mounting holes for a jack stand, fixed or caster wheel. Couplers are manufactured in four generally accepted weight classifications:

CLASS I	2000 lbs. gross
CLASS II	3500 lbs. gross
CLASS III	5000 lbs. gross
CLASS IV	8500 lbs. gross

The gross weight must include the trailer, boat, and all gear carried in the boat. A ball hitch connector is generally not strong enough for loads over 8500 lbs. gross, however, loaded boat trailers are usually under this weight. Be sure to match the coupler used to the gross weight requirements of the boat and trailer being towed.

The device that positively locks the coupler to the ball hitch mounted on the towing vehicle is of three basic locking types. All locking mechanisms work on a similar principle. The coupler has a hollowed out upper portion to accommodate the ball hitch. The lower part is a clamp shaped to fit the underside of the matching ball.

The snap or lever lock type utilizes a handle on the coupler to move the clamp to a lock position. The lever lock is possibly the most foolproof, but it must be locked in position by either a bolt, pin, or padlock.

The hand wheel coupler tightens the clamp around the ball with a spring loaded top hand screw. After tightening the spring, a ratchet system prevents the screw from backing out.

The simplest type, often used by trailer rentals, will fit a variety of ball sizes. Not as common as the other types, it has an upper and lower socket that fits around the ball hitch. The sockets are tightened on the ball by a bolt with a loop handle that is threaded into the lower socket. The safety chain is threaded through this loop to prevent the bolt from backing off and releasing the sockets that fasten the coupler to the ball.

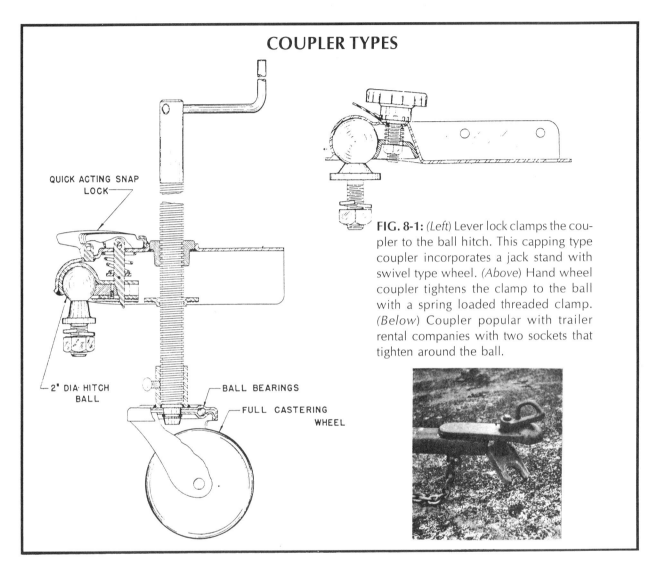

COUPLER TYPES

QUICK ACTING SNAP
LOCK

2" DIA· HITCH
BALL

BALL BEARINGS

FULL CASTERING
WHEEL

FIG. 8-1: (*Left*) Lever lock clamps the coupler to the ball hitch. This capping type coupler incorporates a jack stand with swivel type wheel. (*Above*) Hand wheel coupler tightens the clamp to the ball with a spring loaded threaded clamp. (*Below*) Coupler popular with trailer rental companies with two sockets that tighten around the ball.

The coupler must be fastened securely to the ball so there is little play, but rotates freely without binding. The hand wheel type can be tightened by hand to the desired tension. The lever lock type is preset to accommodate the matching ball, however, a nut on the coupler underside provides tension adjustment.

All of the trailer couplers are simple in operation. They must, however, be kept clean and well oiled if they are to operate satisfactorily. The coupler surfaces that contact the ball must be kept clean. If launching off a sandy beach, the trailer coupler may become clogged with sand that must be removed prior to re-coupling to the towing vehicle. When the screw type is used, care must be taken that it isn't loosened too much; it rotates easily when uncoupled and the lower clamp can come loose and drop in the water during launch or retrieval.

The coupler is most often attached to the trailer tongue by welding, although bolts can be used.

COUPLERS AND ACCESSORIES
(GVW refers to Gross Vehicle Weight)

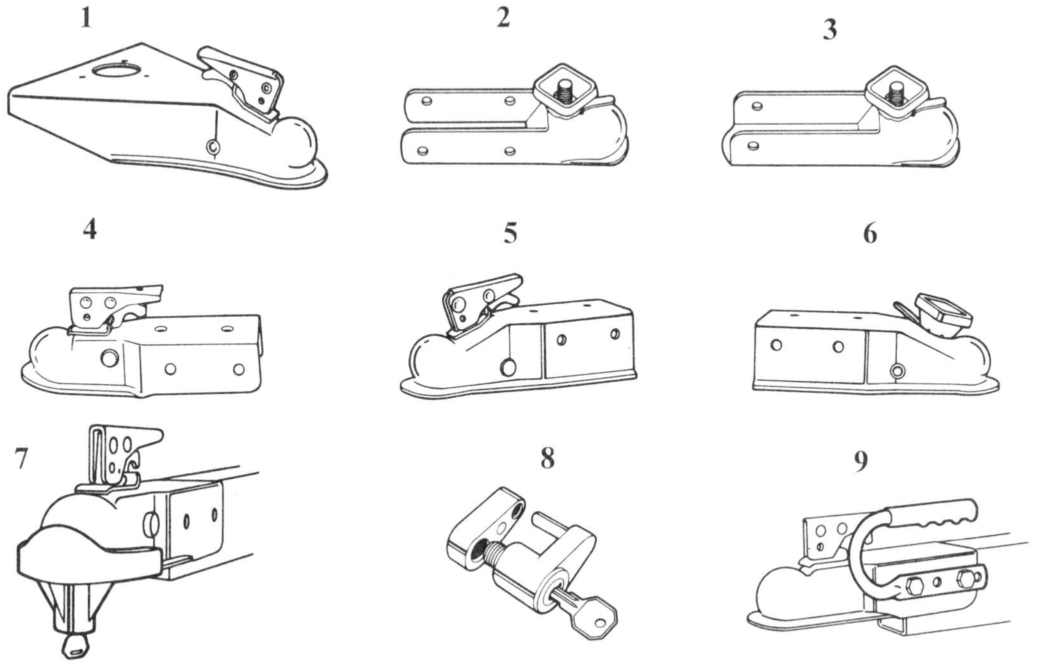

FIG. 8-2: **#1**- Class 3 (5000 GVW), 50°, capping, lever lock, coupler with jack stand mounting holes. **#2**- Class 1 (2000 lbs. GVW) hand wheel, screw type coupler for 2" round pipe trailer tongue. **#3**- As for #2 but for 2 3/8" wide trailer tongue. **#4**- Class 1 (2000 lbs. GVW) or Class 2 (3500 lb. GVW) lever type coupler for 2", 2 1/2", and 3" trailer tongue widths. **#5**- Class 3 (5000 lb. GVW) lever type coupler for 3" tongue width. **#6**- Class 2 (3500 lb. GVW) lever type coupler for 3" tongue width. **#7**- Lock prevents trailer theft; coupler will not accept ball when keyed lock device is attached. **#8**- Keyed hitch lock for lever type couplers prevents theft on or off the vehicle. **#9**- Handy grip handle bolts to side of coupler for easy trailer positioning.

Courtesy FULTON PERFORMANCE PRODUCTS

In either case, the connection should be strong as the coupler is the all-important link that connects the boat trailer to the car. The height of the coupler must be such as to make the boat level when connected to the towing vehicle. Tongue height adjustments can be made in the trailer hitch to some extent, however, some variations are also possible with the coupler. Couplers are available with a gooseneck arrangement that can raise the coupler a few inches above the trailer frame top surface.

A coupler accessory that discourages thefts should be considered if the boat and trailer are parked in unprotected areas. One such device locks the portion of the coupler that accepts the hitch ball; if the coupler can't be coupled to a hitch, the possibility of theft is minimized.   ❖

JACK STANDS

A jack stand is used to lift the trailer off the hitch of the towing vehicle. If the tongue weight is more than can be easily lifted, such an assist is a necessity. The most common type is mounted on the trailer tongue with a caster wheel for moving the trailer around when uncoupled. A jack stand also simplifies raising or lowering the coupler in position when connecting or disconnecting from the ball hitch. The device will eliminate much of the risks of a strained back or smashed fingers when coupling or uncoupling at a slippery launching ramp. FIG. 9-2 illustrates a variety of jack stands that raise or lower the trailer by winding a side or top mounted crank.

Although a swivel wheel jack stand works well when moving the boat on a nicely paved area, the typical launching ramp is not always smooth concrete. Swivel wheels tend to get caught in even minor cavities and the stress on the mounting when trying to force the wheel sideways is tremendous. A swivel wheel must follow the direction the tongue is being pushed or pulled. Trying to move the trailer tongue with the swivel wheel twisted and not tracking is asking for trouble. The higher the trailer tongue is lifted from the ground, the greater the problem. The jack stand with swivel wheel is a great assist, but if abused will fail.

Jack stands are rated by lbs. of capacity but

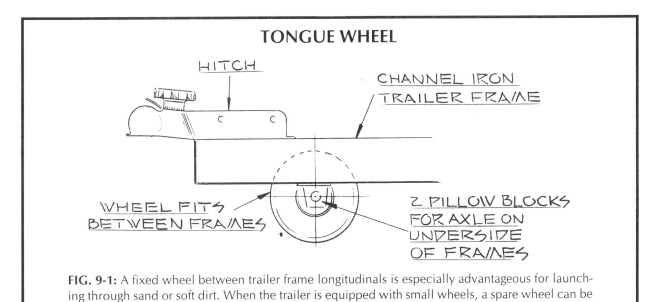

TONGUE WHEEL

HITCH

CHANNEL IRON
TRAILER FRAME

WHEEL FITS
BETWEEN FRAMES

2 PILLOW BLOCKS
FOR AXLE ON
UNDERSIDE
OF FRAMES

FIG. 9-1: A fixed wheel between trailer frame longitudinals is especially advantageous for launching through sand or soft dirt. When the trailer is equipped with small wheels, a spare wheel can be mounted in this manner and serve a dual purpose.

how to build boat trailers

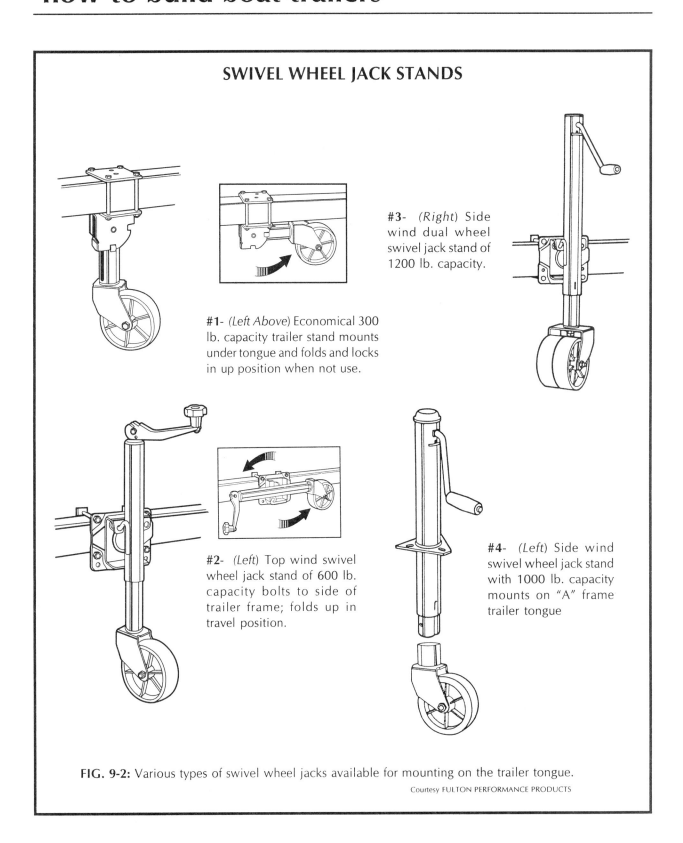

SWIVEL WHEEL JACK STANDS

#3- *(Right)* Side wind dual wheel swivel jack stand of 1200 lb. capacity.

#1- *(Left Above)* Economical 300 lb. capacity trailer stand mounts under tongue and folds and locks in up position when not use.

#2- *(Left)* Top wind swivel wheel jack stand of 600 lb. capacity bolts to side of trailer frame; folds up in travel position.

#4- *(Left)* Side wind swivel wheel jack stand with 1000 lb. capacity mounts on "A" frame trailer tongue

FIG. 9-2: Various types of swivel wheel jacks available for mounting on the trailer tongue.

Courtesy FULTON PERFORMANCE PRODUCTS

'BUILD YOUR OWN' SWIVEL WHEEL STAND

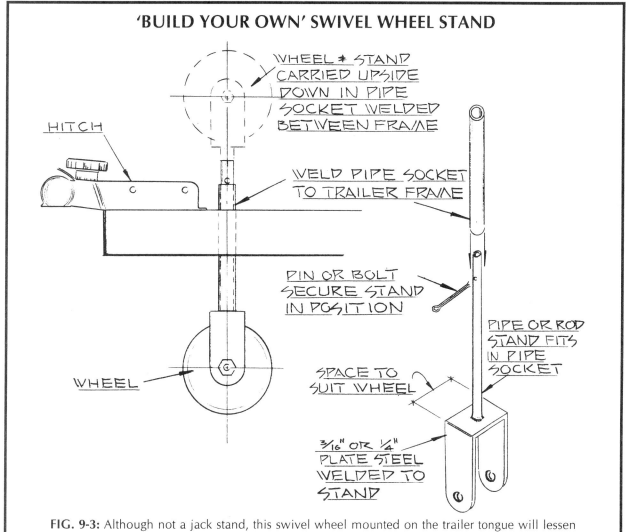

WHEEL & STAND CARRIED UPSIDE DOWN IN PIPE SOCKET WELDED BETWEEN FRAME

HITCH

WELD PIPE SOCKET TO TRAILER FRAME

PIN OR BOLT SECURE STAND IN POSITION

WHEEL

PIPE OR ROD STAND FITS IN PIPE SOCKET

SPACE TO SUIT WHEEL

3/16" OR 1/4" PLATE STEEL WELDED TO STAND

FIG. 9-3: Although not a jack stand, this swivel wheel mounted on the trailer tongue will lessen the chore of moving the boat around the storage area or during launching and retrieving the boat from the trailer.

this figure undoubtedly doesn't take into account the stresses that may occur in typical boat launching and retrieval. It's best to use an assembly with a far higher rating than the actual trailer tongue weight.

Trailer jack stands are available with various mountings. They may mount under or to the side of a frame member or the tongue. A unit that mounts on the trailer centerline as far forward as possible is preferable for anything but light trailer/boat combinations.

The "build your own" shown in FIG. 9-3 is a swivel type wheel that slips into a socket after lifting the trailer manually from the towing vehicle trailer hitch. When not is use, it may be inverted to become readily accessible and yet be out of the way.

Jack stand casters or wheels are not intended for use on sandy or undeveloped ramps, which becomes readily apparent if you try it. However, regardless of the area you will be moving the trailer on, some type of tongue wheel is desirable for retrieving or launching a boat, even if the tongue weight can be readily handled. A non pivoting wheel such as shown in FIG. 9-1 is ideal and quite simple to make. The spare tire and dolly bracket for a small wheeled trailer can be mounted in a similar manner to make use of the spare in launching and retrieving (see FIG. 9-4). If launching through sand or soft dirt, a wide tire and wheel is preferable; if the wheel is air-filled, deflating the tire to minimum pressure is also helpful.

When launching and retrieving through soft sand, a wide skid is often more desirable than a forward wheel, as it will not sink into the sand as far. A skid can be made from flatbar or sheet stock welded under the trailer tongue as far forward as possible, but located so as not interfere with the coupler. The skid is generally "U" shape, of adequate depth to keep the coupler clear of the ground when the trailer is

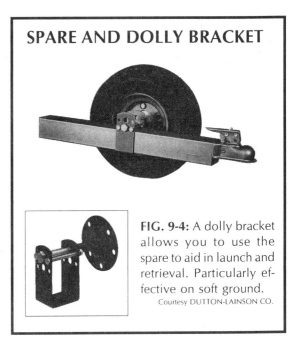

SPARE AND DOLLY BRACKET

FIG. 9-4: A dolly bracket allows you to use the spare to aid in launch and retrieval. Particularly effective on soft ground.
Courtesy DUTTON-LAINSON CO.

moved fore or aft. The width can vary, however, if going through sand or silt, a wider skid will have less tendency to sink in and thus be easier to maneuver during launch and retrieval. Tongue weight is minor on small trailers and thus they may be readily moved around on a skid almost as easily as with a forward wheel. A skid can be incorporated with a jack stand and caster wheel that folds up when not in use, for the best of both worlds. ❖

10

BOAT FORMS

The purpose of forms on a boat trailer is to cradle the boat, as nearly as possible, as it will be supported in the water. Since the average trailer boat spends most of its life on a trailer, the cradle or form is all important. The bottom of an improperly or inadequately supported boat can quickly become distorted. There are many instances of boats operating satisfactorily when first purchased or built, that developed a warped bottom after being inadequately supported on the trailer. This in turn drastically altered the riding and handling characteristics. It is important that the trailer frame be be strong and ridgid enough to support the forms without movement. If the trailer frame is too light, it may deflect in such a manner that the forms will not properly support the boat. If an aft form can be stepped on and forced away from the boat bottom easily, the frame of the trailer does not have the necessary rigidity to properly support the forms. In this case, reinforcing the trailer frame with either a truss, as shown in Chapter 7, FIG. 7-3, or other stiffening methods is imperative. In the following paragraphs, three types of commonly used boat supports will be discussed: rollers, longitudinal, and athwartship forms.

ROLLERS

Many manufacturers of ready-built trailers use rollers to cradle the boat. Rollers have a dis-

tinct advantage on tilt-bed or even a fixed form trailers, as it is much easier to launch and retrieve the trailer without getting the wheel bearings wet. A common problem is that too few or inadequately placed rollers are used. The use of an insufficient number of rollers tends to distort the boat, as described in the previous paragraph. Stock "standard" trailers usually have several rollers located along the keel and few along the chine (junction of the side and bottom of the boat). The problem occurs when trailing the vehicle around sharp curves and the weight of the boat is thrown almost entirely on one side, which in the extreme, can punch a hole in the bottom of a lightly constructed boat. Distortion of the boat bottom also occurs when the boat rests on a small roller area for a long period. For this reason, except on very lightweight boats, rollers are seldom used as the sole supports to cradle the boat.

Properly set up rollers support the boat uniformly. Each roller should be adjusted to evenly distribute the load. Rollers along the keel are preferably located directly under the centerline of the boat, under the outer skeg or keel. Heavy, wide, large diameter rollers should be used near the transom, particularly when an outboard or stern mounted inboard boat is to be trailered. Rollers outboard the centerline should be as wide and as large in diameter as possible. Along the chine, rollers should spaced a maximum of three feet apart. The photos, FIG. 10-2, show numerous roller combina-

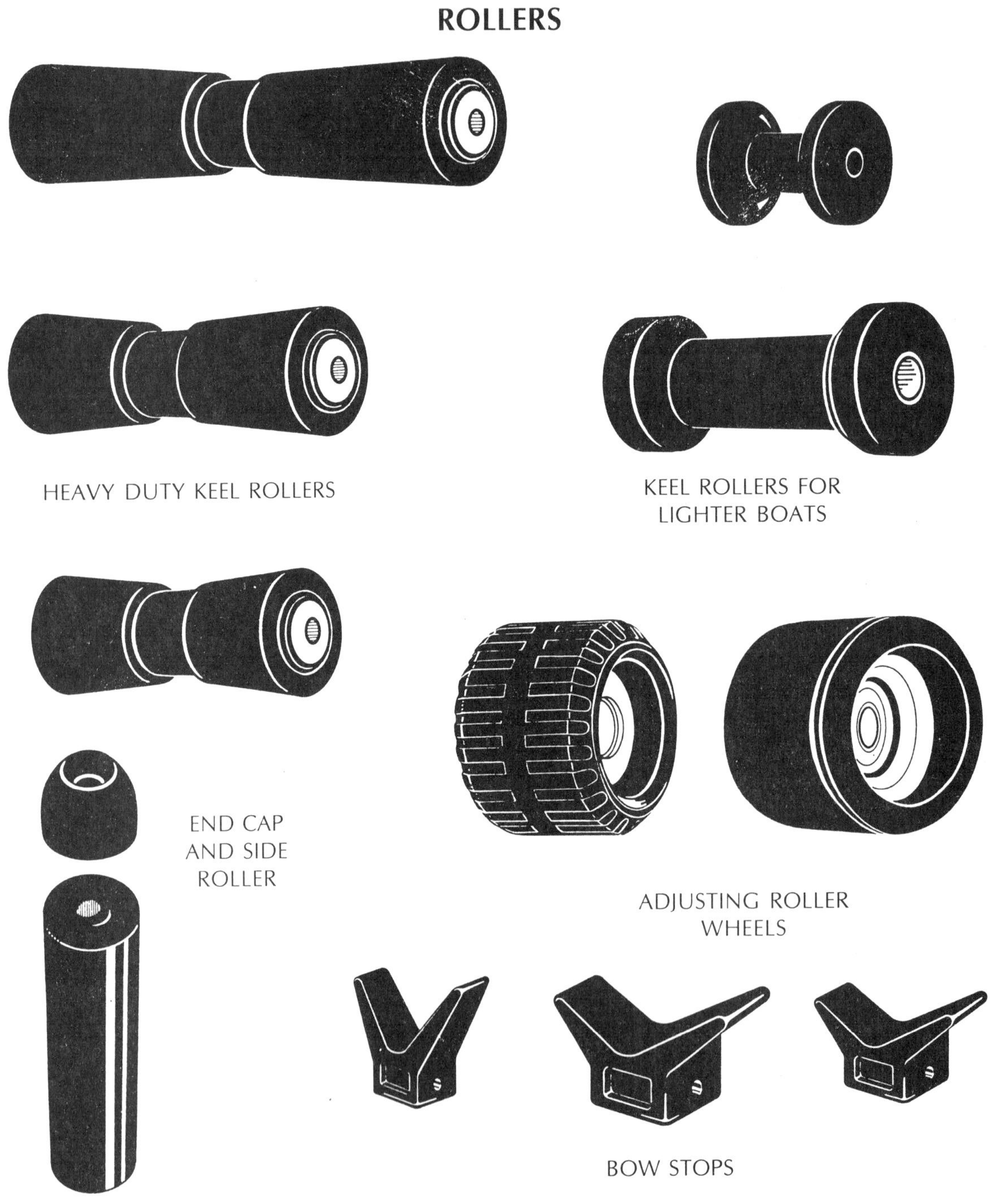

ROLLERS

HEAVY DUTY KEEL ROLLERS

KEEL ROLLERS FOR
LIGHTER BOATS

END CAP
AND SIDE
ROLLER

ADJUSTING ROLLER
WHEELS

BOW STOPS

FIG. 10-1: Many types of molded rollers are available to accommodate most boat trailer requirements.

Courtesy B&M MANUFACTURING CO.

FIG. 10-2: Various types of rollers used as boat cradles: **#1-** Typical roller used along the keel. **#2** and **#3-** Other types of keel rollers; most will have a slight vee or ridges to track the boat in place on the trailer centerline. **#4-** A combination of keel rollers and longitudinal bunks at the chine. **#5-** Roller keel supports with a series of rollers to support the hull at the chine. **#6-** The upright transom guides are roller equipped. **#7** and **#8-** Several centerline rollers are used to start the boat on the trailer during retrieval. **#9-** Three rollers positioned to accommodate the forward vee bottomed boat.

tions, both good and bad, that will provide ideas for the proper combinations for your boat trailer. All rollers should be lubricated frequently and checked to make sure they roll easily and have not shifted.

LIFTING BUNK/ROLLER COMBINATION

An unusual combination of fixed longitudinal bunks, which support the boat with special rollers that act as eccentrics to lift the boat from the cradle, is illustrated in FIG. 10-3. This method is unusual in that it gives the boat full support by the use of bunks, yet allows the boat to be readily raised on rollers, which in this case are wide-tread wheels. In the particular instance shown, the boat is 19' with a gross weight of approximately 2300 lbs., which includes boat, motor, and load. Only four of the wheels are used, but they are strategically located under heavy longitudinal members. The system has been in use for several seasons and has not given any problems or shown any tendency to distort the bottom while launching. The system operates by pivoting the wheels with a long handle or extension bar used by a person on either side of the boat. Working together with a lever arm about 42" long, two people can lift the boat on either end without undue effort. The boat is wholly supported by the wheels and thus can be rolled on or off the trailer with ease.

One manufacturer uses a similar method of a combination of rollers and longitudinal bunks only in reverse; that is, the boat is carried on

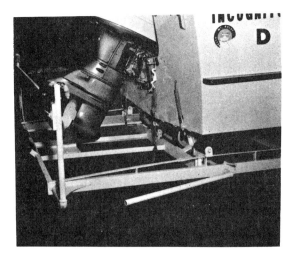

FIG. 10-3: Example of a mechanism that raises the rollers to the bottom of the boat when ready for launching. (see text) #B and C: The bow and stern rollers do not contact the bottom when the boat is being transported. #D: Lever action is used to bring the rollers in contact with the boat bottom for launching or retrieving.

longitudinal bunks or supports when being trailed. When the boat is readied for launching, the forms are lowered by leverage, much as described in the previous paragraph, until the boat contacts a series of rollers. After retrieving the boat to the trailer, the forms are raised to support the boat for trailering.

ATHWARTSHIP BOAT FORMS

Fixed forms, running athwartship or across the boat, were almost universally used at the outset of trailer boating. Still practical for larger boats, sailboats, and those of irregular bottom contour, athwartship forms are usually cut from 2" thick wooden members that are carefully fitted to the bottom of the boat. These forms are best mounted directly under an athwartship frame on a wooden boat. The contour, thus, may be taken directly from the frame member. Most fiberglass and many aluminum boats do not have athwartship frames and thus are better supported by longitudinal forms. Athwartship forms must be carefully adjusted to equally divide the weight of the boat over the various supports. It is imperative that the aft form be directly under the transom; leaving the boat overhanging to any degree may cause a hook (indentation just forward of the transom) to be forced into the bottom of the hull. This is especially true for outboard or inboard/outdrive powered boats where the major weight is located at the transom; athwartship forms in the aft section should extend completely across the boat. A partial form supporting the boat at the keel is usually used toward the bow of the typical vee bottomed craft. Athwartship supports can be used in conjunction with other types of forms, such as longitudinal bunks and rollers.

LONGITUDINAL FORMS OR BUNKS

Longitudinal forms, or bunks as they are often called, give the most uniform support to the boat. They have become increasingly popular with high-performance boats, both inboards and outboards. This type of form gives more bearing surface to support the bottom of the boat. The chances of the boat bottom being distorted when carried or stored on the trailer is minimized when the load is spread over larger areas.

If the boat bottom is relatively flat, the longitudinals may be simple 2" x 6" or 2" x 4" members, padded with carpet or similar material. If, however, the bottom has any fore and aft sweep, it may be necessary to use longitudinal forms somewhat like those used athwartship; sawn to shape to match the bottom curvature.

Longitudinal bunks can be laminated to shape over the bottom of an inverted boat. Be sure to lay a sheet of plastic film over the bottom to protect it while laminating the 1" x 4" (or other size that will make the bend easily) longitudinals. Three or more laminates are required, glued together with epoxy or similar marine adhesive. Hold the laminates to the boat bottom with weights; plastic bags filled with sand work well. When working in a garage or other structure, the laminates can be held to the boat bottom by braces from rafters or other overhead building members. Athwartship forms or steel brackets are used to mount the molded longitudinal to the trailer frame. This type of boat cradle is a lot of work, but the resultant form will greatly reduce the possibility of hull damage.

CROSS FORMS

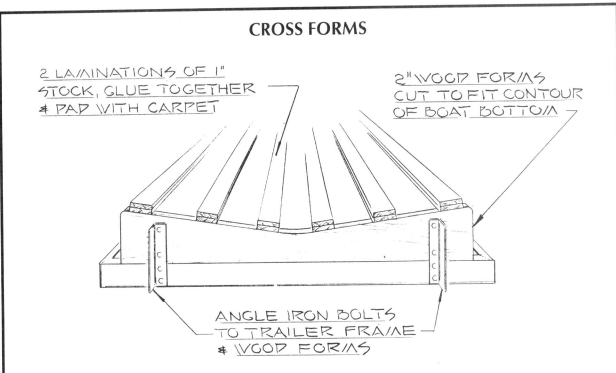

2 LAMINATIONS OF 1"
STOCK, GLUE TOGETHER
& PAD WITH CARPET

2" WOOD FORMS
CUT TO FIT CONTOUR
OF BOAT BOTTOM

ANGLE IRON BOLTS
TO TRAILER FRAME
& WOOD FORMS

FIG. 10-4: Cross supports may be used alone, as shown below, or in combination with longitudinal forms or bunks as depicted above.

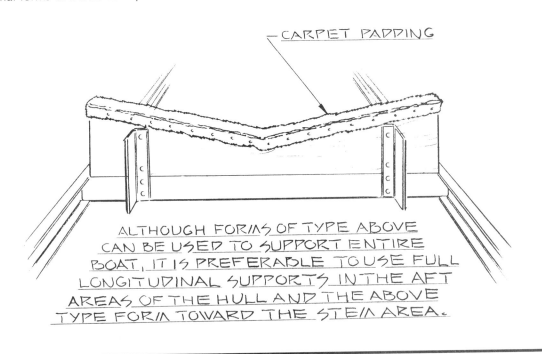

CARPET PADDING

ALTHOUGH FORMS OF TYPE ABOVE
CAN BE USED TO SUPPORT ENTIRE
BOAT, IT IS PREFERABLE TO USE FULL
LONGITUDINAL SUPPORTS IN THE AFT
AREAS OF THE HULL AND THE ABOVE
TYPE FORM TOWARD THE STEM AREA.

BUNK ADJUSTMENT

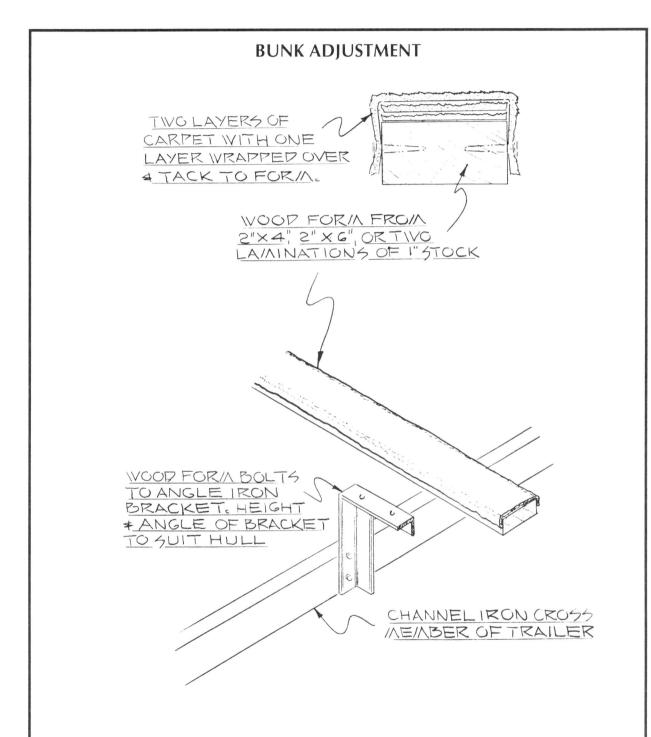

TWO LAYERS OF CARPET WITH ONE LAYER WRAPPED OVER & TACK TO FORM.

WOOD FORM FROM 2"X4", 2" X 6", OR TWO LAMINATIONS OF 1" STOCK

WOOD FORM BOLTS TO ANGLE IRON BRACKET. HEIGHT & ANGLE OF BRACKET TO SUIT HULL

CHANNEL IRON CROSS MEMBER OF TRAILER

FIG. 10-5: Bunks should be well padded and adjusted to fit firmly and uniformly to the boat bottom. The steel angle brackets can be moved up and down against the trailer frame until the form mates to the boat bottom; then through bolted in place.

Padding for the forms may be carpeting; rubber stripping, fabric fire hose, or on larger boats, strips of automotive tires. Padding is not meant to cushion the boat but to prevent chafing the finish. Regardless of the tie down method, a minor movement will occur between the boat and the forms.

COMBINATION BOAT SUPPORTS

A combination of boat supports, rollers, athwartship cradles, and longitudinal bunks can be used to provide adequate support and take advantage of each. Many commercially available boat trailers use a combination of at least two of these support methods. The choice will depend largely on the launching conditions and boat being trailed. A series of rollers supporting a heavy inboard powered hull is a poor choice; longitudinal bunks are ideal. A small sailboat could be cradled by rollers but a few wider supports, bunks, or athwartship cradles are advised. When launching conditions require submerging the trailer wheels and the boat is floated off the trailer, rollers may not be necessary. Because boaters are likely to trail their boat to areas that may have a variety of launching conditions, multiple support methods may be desirable.

BOW SUPPORTS

FIGS. 10-6, 10-7, and 10-8 illustrate several types of support for the bow; these may be used with or without a winch. Padded bow forms used on commercial trailers are adjustable to various positions to suit a variety of boats.

The bow support illustrated in FIG. 10-6 is

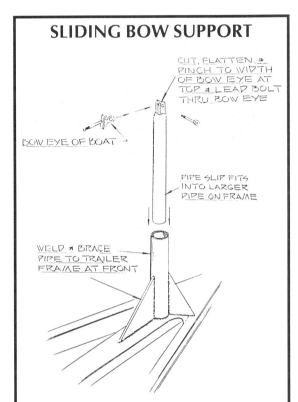

SLIDING BOW SUPPORT

FIG. 10-6: A bow support that is ideal for launching or retrieval from submerged trailers. During retrieval the inner pipe support holds the bow of the boat in position; as the boat and trailer are retrieved, the inner pipe slides inside the outer one. A pin through both pipes or other tie down should be provided during traveling to lock the boat to the supports.

ideal for heavier boats. This method uses an upper pipe sliding inside another one that is fastened securely to the trailer. This arrangement simplifies retrieving the boat from the water and positioning it at the bow. The upper pipe slides up far enough to fasten to the bow eye. When the boat is pulled from the water, the pipe slides down in position and locates the bow of the boat properly. A pin or bolt through the two pipes locks them together in the down position and secures the boat at the bow.

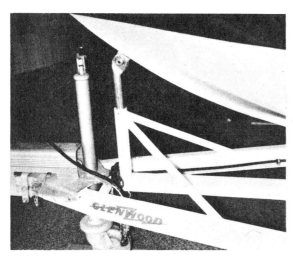 

FIG. 10-7: (*Left*) A bow support similar to that shown in Fig. 10-6 used on a 17' boat with inboard stern mounted motor. (*Right*) A pivoting arm that also keeps the boat in position during retrieval. A secure tie down or method of locking the bow securely to the trailer when the boat is being trailered should be used with this pivoting bow support.

BOW SUPPORTS

WINCH NOT USED

SLOT FOR BOW EYE WITH PADDING. BOLT GOES THRU BOW EYE TO SECURE BOAT TO TRAILER

BRACE AS REQUIRED

CHANNEL OR TWO PIECES OF ANGLE IRON

FIG. 10-8: (*Top*) The boat bow eye, slipped through a steel bracket welded to the trailer, securely locks the boat in place. (*Bottom*) A bow support method that can be used in conjunction with a winch. A secure method of anchoring the boat to the trailer bow support should be provided.

WINCH STAND LEVEL WITH BOW EYE

¼" X 1" X 4" FLAT PLATE BOLTED TO CHANNEL. ADDITIONAL HOLES MAY BE DRILLED FOR ADJUSTMENT

ROD BENT TO SHAPE OF BOW. SLIP RUBBER HOSE OVER FOR PADDING. STOCK RUBBER BOW PIECE OPTIONAL

67

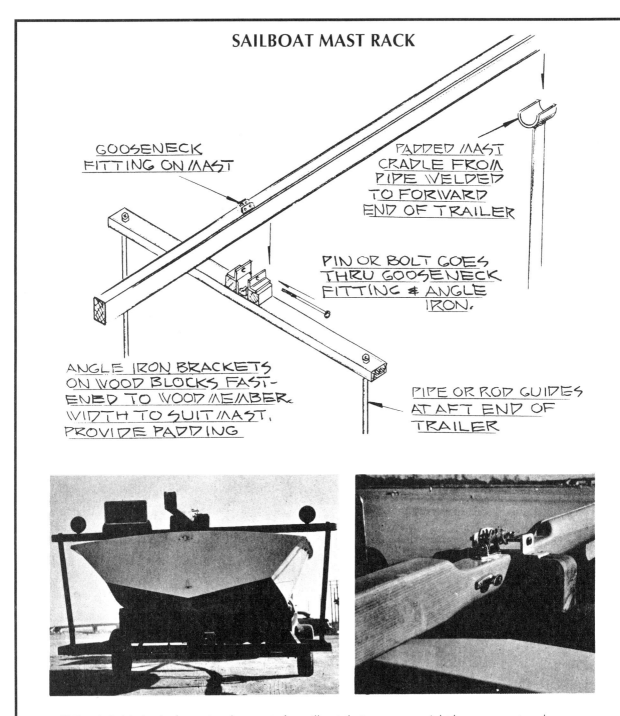

SAILBOAT MAST RACK

GOOSENECK FITTING ON MAST

PADDED MAST CRADLE FROM PIPE WELDED TO FORWARD END OF TRAILER

PIN OR BOLT GOES THRU GOOSENECK FITTING & ANGLE IRON.

ANGLE IRON BRACKETS ON WOOD BLOCKS FASTENED TO WOOD MEMBER. WIDTH TO SUIT MAST, PROVIDE PADDING

PIPE OR ROD GUIDES AT AFT END OF TRAILER

FIG. 10-9: Method of carrying the mast of a sailboat that uses an upright bow support and removable light bar to cradle the spar. (*Lower right*) The mast gooseneck fitting is used to anchor the spar to the aft form.

A winch should not be used as the primary tie down at the bow. This is common practice, but the boat should be held firmly at the bow by additional means. When a winch rope is used as an added hold down the following procedure is advised: Double the winch line, slip it through the bow eye, and loop it over a hook on one side of the winch stand. Secure the winch cable hook to the other side of the winch stand. When the winch is tightened up, it will hold the boat forward and down at the same time. The vertical height of the winch must match the bow eye of the boat. Typical heights of the bow eye on the boat are 16" above an extension of the keel line for boats under 16', and 20" above the keel line for boats over 16'.

TIE DOWNS

Gravity alone isn't enough to keep a boat firmly on a trailer, and a boat bouncing up and down on a trailer can cause severe damage to the hull. Locking the boat at the bow and expecting guides or uprights to keep the boat on the trailer isn't enough. Experienced trailer boaters prefer transom hold downs and athwartship straps in addition to the bow tie down.

Athwartship or gunwale tie downs straps are good insurance. These straps start at one side trailer frame member and go across the gunwales to the opposite side of the trailer frame. A tie down that tightens by a cam action leverage system is preferable. Be sure that athwartship straps are wide and well padded as they go across the gunwales; chafing can quickly wear the boat finish.

Transom tie downs on smaller boats are typically adjustable straps that hook over the boat transom and trailer frame. A chain or cable tie down with a turnbuckle for tightening adjustment is preferable for heavier boats. FIG. 10-10 illustrates a transom hold down method that uses the aft vertical guides welded to the trailer to secure the boat. These upright guides are minimum 3/4" pipe with the threaded portion of a bolt slipped in the top and welded in place. An athwartship, form with holes on either end to match those of the uprights, slides up and down the pipe. The form is tightened down by nuts on the upright threaded pipes. Obviously, the upper portion of the uprights must be vertical and parallel to allow the form to adjust up and down freely. The form may be a flat padded 2" x 4" on smaller boats where the contact is primarily at the gunwale. A boat with a crowned aft deck will require a heavier cut-to-shape athwartship form, well padded to prevent marring the finish. A hold down form of this type holds the boat securely to the trailer and can also hold the license plate, and the stop, tail, and turn signal lights. When ready to launch, the form can be removed so the lights do not contact water.

SAILBOAT FORMS

Trailer forms to carry small centerboard boats may be similar to those used for outboard powered craft. Additional rollers or forms are desirable beneath the centerboard trunk opening if the board is metal or heavily weighted. A centerboard that projects through the bottom when in the up position should be cradled with a central longitudinal on the trailer frame.

Swing keel sailboats or those with a shallow appendage beneath the bottom of the boat are supported primarily along the centerline di-

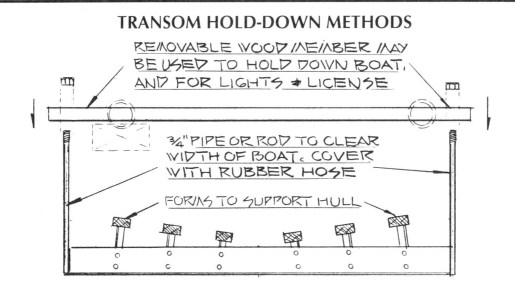

TRANSOM HOLD-DOWN METHODS

REMOVABLE WOOD MEMBER MAY
BE USED TO HOLD DOWN BOAT,
AND FOR LIGHTS & LICENSE

¾" PIPE OR ROD TO CLEAR
WIDTH OF BOAT. COVER
WITH RUBBER HOSE

FORMS TO SUPPORT HULL

AFT VIEW OF TRAILER

FIG. 10-10: (*Top*) A removable cross member holds the boat firmly to the cradle and may be used as a light bar. (*Bottom*) Turnbuckles or heavy web straps from transom eyes to trailer frame provide a positive method of anchoring the boat to the supporting cradle.

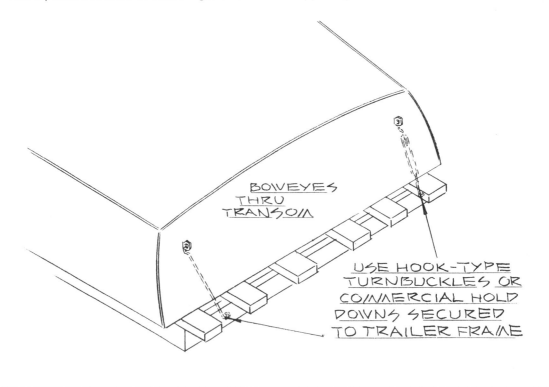

BOW EYES
THRU
TRANSOM

USE HOOK-TYPE
TURNBUCKLES OR
COMMERCIAL HOLD
DOWNS SECURED
TO TRAILER FRAME

rectly under the keel. See FIG. 10-12. The keel rests on a padded form, often fastened to a central member on the trailer frame, while athwartship or longitudinal forms support and hold the sailboat upright. The keel appendage should slide free from the trailer without going over cross trailer frame members. Vertical padding along the trailer frame keel slot is re-

quired to prevent damage to the finish and guide the sailboat keel appendage to a solid padded form on the trailer frame.

A full or fin keel sailboat is difficult to launch and retrieve and the forms required are more complex. Where available, most boat owners will prefer a launch by a crane and sling. Dur-

FIG. 10-11: (*Top*) Excellent example of longitudinal bunks used to support an inboard boat with relatively flat bottom. (*Left*) Forward cross form used to support the vee'd bow of the boat. (*Right*) Trailer for a catamaran with flat runners. Fenders are padded but some other method should be used to prevent the boat from sliding

SAILBOAT TRAILERS

FIG. 10-12: (*Top Left and Right*) Trailers for sailboats that have moderate underwater keel appendages. The primary support is under the keel with longitudinal bunks cradling the hull. (*Center Left and Right*) The trailer to the left has numerous well braced vertical supports to accommodate a keeled 23' sailboat. The trailer on the right is for a much lighter and smaller craft requiring minimal supports. (*Bottom Left*) Trailer for a 28' keeled sailboat with numerous supports rigidly braced to the trailer frame.

Courtesy TRAIL-RITE

OUTBOARD MOTOR BRACE

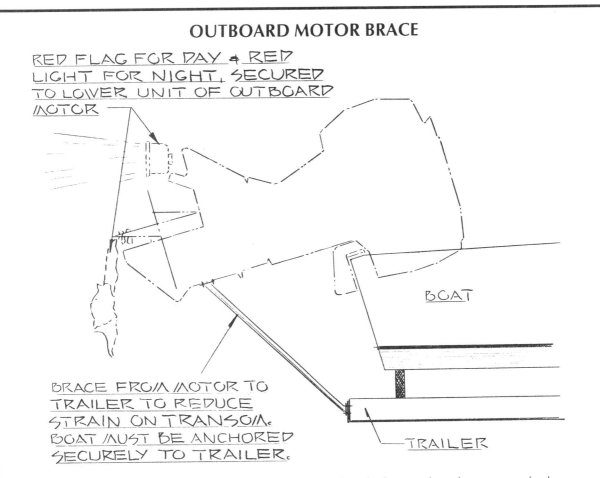

RED FLAG FOR DAY & RED
LIGHT FOR NIGHT, SECURED
TO LOWER UNIT OF OUTBOARD
MOTOR

BOAT

BRACE FROM MOTOR TO
TRAILER TO REDUCE
STRAIN ON TRANSOM.
BOAT MUST BE ANCHORED
SECURELY TO TRAILER.

TRAILER

FIG. 10-13: (*Above*) A build it yourself support for the tilted up outboard motor, used when traveling to lessen the strain on the boat transom. (*Below*) Commercially available shock absorbing outboard motor support bracket cushions road shocks and vibration.

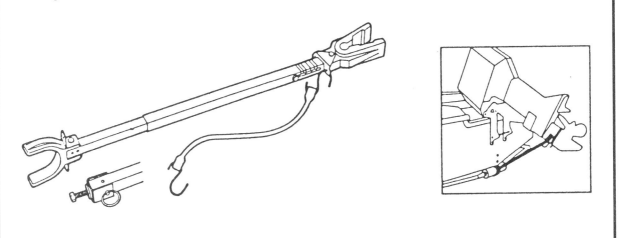

ing a ramp launch or retrieval of a keel sailboat, the trailer is most often completely submerged and even with a relatively steep slope almost impossible to launch without in-the-water help. Trailer tongue extensions and/or using the tidal launch methods described in Chapter 14 are helpful, but it is usually necessary to have someone on hand in a swim suit when launching a keeled sailboat.

A solid form trailer frame member, or support directly under the weighted keel, is the best primary support for this type of sailboat. The ballasted keel is heavily built and can usually support the entire boat weight without causing structural problems. Forms to support the boat and keep it in the upright position are braced by steel structural members. Forms or pads connected to pipes that slide inside another vertical pipe welded through the trailer frame provide adjustment. Since a major portion of the sailboat weight is carried by the keel support, the major function of the forms is to keep the boat upright. However, a tremendous strain is incurred when a tall load makes a sharp turn even at a relatively slow speed. The low center of gravity, because of the weighted keel, helps to maintain balance, but support forms should be rigidly braced.

Sailboats that are to be trailered have a rather complex problem with spars. Where possible, the boom can be carried on the trailer, but most often the mast is so long that a special carrying rack is necessary. One method of carrying the longer masts is illustrated in FIG. 10-9. The forward support is an upright welded to the trailer bed with a cradle on top. The aft support can be mounted on a form supported by uprights, described in the section on "Tie

Downs". An aft mast support can also be located in the boat cockpit if the spar is not too long. Care must be taken that the forward overhang of the mast does not hit the towing vehicle when going over dips. This especially holds true when a van, station wagon, or a camper truck is the towing vehicle. The amount of overhang aft of the boat and trailer is limited by law and should be checked with local authorities in the state where the rig will be trailed. Lights and/or a red flag is desirable on any overhang load and may be required by state law.

OUTBOARD MOTOR SUPPORT

Trailer boats powered by outboard motors create special problems. The outboard motor creates a tremendous stress on the transom during trailering. If the motor is left in the down position, the lower unit will usually scrape when going down a driveway or incline. When tilted up, the stress on the transom is considerable. If the outboard is held in the up position by locking the tilt mechanism it can be jarred free going over a bump. Be sure a positive method is used to prevent the outboard from tilting back and forth during trailering.

A support from the trailer chassis to the lower unit of the outboard motor is highly desirable, particularly with larger outboard motors. Such a unit, illustrated in FIG. 10-13, can be custom made and fitted to the trailer to hold the motor firmly to the trailer forms. A bouncing outboard motor can cause serious, often unrepairable damage to the boat. Many boat trailer companies and accessory suppliers have adjustable supports that fit most motor and trailer combinations. ❖

WINCHES

A winch is used to control the speed of the boat as it slides from a trailer during launching, and provides a mechanical advantage to more easily retrieve the boat from the water and reposition it on the trailer. Winches have the ability to move a much heavier boat than would be possible with manpower; with the turn of a handle for a manual winch, or actuating a switch for an electric type.

The connection from the bow eye of the boat to the winch is generally cable (wire rope), synthetic rope, or web strap, and most often is not supplied with a manually operated winch. The reel capacity will vary depending on the type of connecting line, an important consideration if launching conditions require a long line. The strength of the coupling line should equal or exceed the strength rating of the winch. A snap hook or similar connection is desirable to easily couple to and uncouple from the boat bow eye.

A winch will only be as efficient as the rollers that support the boat will allow. Seldom are winches practical for launching or retrieving heavy boats that are supported solely on the trailer by bunks or fixed forms. The launching procedure and retrieval for such a trailer/boat combination requires floating the boat off the trailer. This usually means someone in the water and/or submerging the trailer entirely and disconnecting it from the tow vehicle. When a boat being retrieved from the water is afloat, pulling the boat to the trailer bow support requires little effort. However, as the boat ceases to float and rests on the trailer, the force required to pull the boat to the bow support increases. Without a winch and proper roller support, a half buoyant boat of any size will be difficult to fully retrieve. Even retrieving small boats with a winch will be simplified with rollers for the boat support. Rollers that are properly located, wide and with large diameters and properly maintained will make retrieval easier. Only with such a balanced roller cradle for the boat will the use of a winch be practical and desirable. (See Chapter 10, "Rollers".)

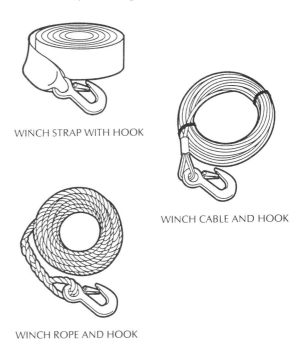

WINCH STRAP WITH HOOK

WINCH CABLE AND HOOK

WINCH ROPE AND HOOK

how to build boat trailers

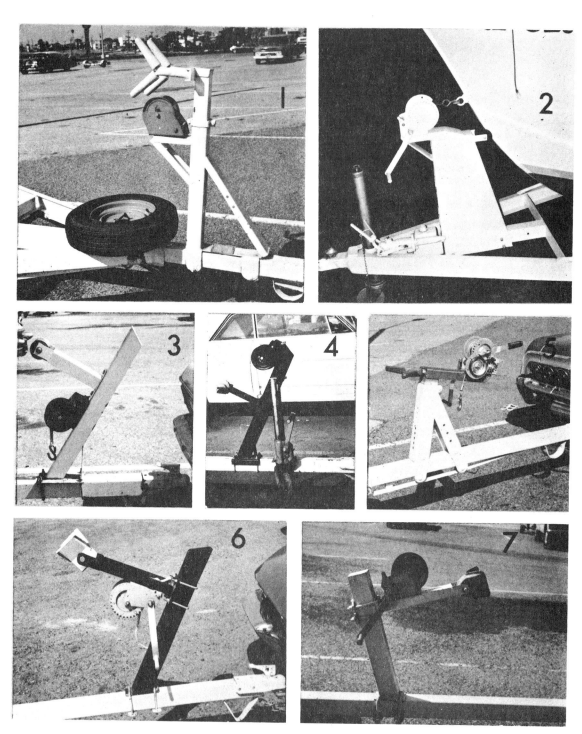

FIG. 11-1: Various methods of mounting the winch to the trailer tongue and providing adequate support for the bow of the boat. The bow support shown in **#1** is designed to support the top edge of the deck/stem junction on a power catamaran. **#2**-The winch stand is reinforced with sheet metal to withstand the forces when launching or retrieving this heavy power cruiser.

WINCH MOUNTING

COMPONENTS

Boat trailer winch components should be matched as follows:
1. The winch rope breaking strength should not be less than 150% of the rated winch capacity.
2. The winch hook breaking strength should not be less than 200% of the rope breaking strength.

RECOMMENDED PRACTICE FOR WINCH MOUNTING PLATE

The hole pattern indicated for the winch mounting plate is compatable with all winches known to be available for boat trailers. The use of this hole pattern should allow any winch to fit the winch stand.
1. The winch mounting plate should be of sufficient rigidity to prevent misalignment of the winch's gear train while under the full load.
2. The winch should be fastened to the mounting plate with 3/8" bolts and nuts.
3. Winches with dimensions greater than 3" between frame sides should be bolted to the mounting plate at a minimum of 3 points for maximum torsional strength. Bolts should pass through the winch base as close to the frame sides as practical.

WINCH LOCATION

Winches should be positioned in line with the bow eye, that is, a maximum of 16" from the extended keel line for boats up to and including 16' in length; a maximum of 20" from the keel line for boats over 16' in length.

WINCH BASE DIMENSIONS

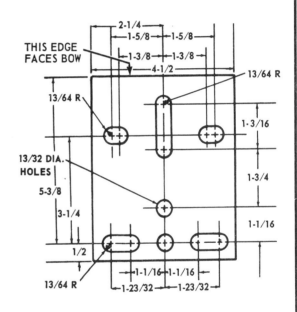

FIG. 11-2

WINCH STAND

The winch must be anchored solidly to the trailer frame with upright winch stand members strong enough and braced in such a manner to withstand the stresses of pulling a boat on a trailer. The photos in FIG. 11-1 illustrate several different types of winch stands commonly used.

The base mounting dimensions of winches are for the most part standardized (FIG. 11-2). Adjust the winch height until the winch cable or strap leads horizontally to the bow eye without interfering with the bow stop. Winches are not intended to hold the boat on the trailer, although many use them for this purpose. A separate tie down is preferable to securely anchor the boat to the trailer. Several methods

how to build boat trailers

are shown in Chapter 10.

MANUAL WINCHES

Manual winch manufacturers offer a wide range of gear ratios, handle lengths, and drum sizes. All of these factors affect the speed, effort required, and the weight that can be pulled or load capacity. The load capacity is stamped on the winch body and specified in the manufacturer's literature. A good rule of thumb is that the maximum gross weight of the boat should not exceed three times the winch rating.

Winches for retrieving boats from the water and pulling them on the trailer are available in various sizes to gain a mechanical advantage. Single speed winches are the least expensive, and may be geared to as small a ratio as 2:1 or 3:1. These are satisfactory for the smaller craft, but most boaters will probably prefer a winch with a greater mechanical advantage. Single speed winches will have less reel capacity meaning the cable or rope length will be shorter.

For heavy-duty use, a gear ratio from 9:1 to 15:1 or more is preferable. Two speed manual winches are similar to the single

TYPICAL WINCHES

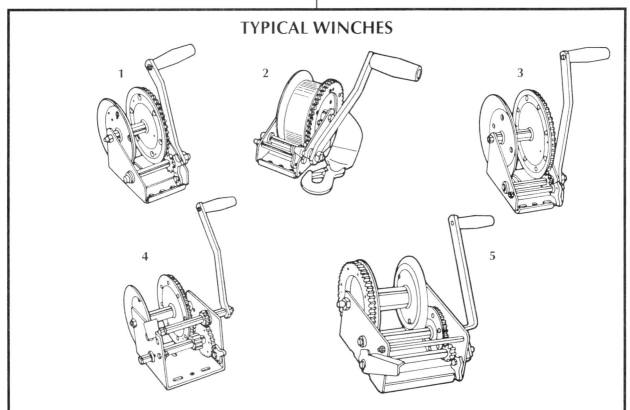

FIG. 11-3: #1- Winch for 900 lbs. capacity 3.1: 1 gear ratio with one way ratchet. **#2**- Winch with 1400 lbs. capacity 4.4:1 gear ratio and two way ratchet. **#3**- Winch with 1800 lbs. capacity 5.1:1 gear ratio and two way ratchet. **#4**- Winch with 2000 lbs. capacity and dual ratio 4.1:1 for quick retrieval and 9.8:1 for heavy loads; free wheels without handle spinning. **#5**- Winch with 3700 lbs. capacity, dual ratio 5.1:1 and 15.8:1 and hand brake. Courtesy FULTON PERFORMANCE PRODUCTS

INCREASING WINCH PULLING POWER

FIG. 11-4: Pulley arrangement on a power winch that increases the pulling capacity.

speed type but have a high speed gear for fast cranking under light load and a low speed gear for slower but greater pulling power. The effort required to winch a boat on a trailer increases as the boat comes closer to the winch; more of the boat is out of the water and friction on the supports is greater. When the effort to turn the winch handle becomes excessive, the winch can be shifted to the higher gear ratio. This results in a slower retrieve but provides greater mechanical advantage and thus requires less effort to operate. Additional mechanical advantage on either an electric or hand winch can be gained by a sheave that attaches to the bow eye of the boat, as shown in FIG. 11-4. Hand winches may have a free wheeling feature that is ideal for launching(the spool turns but the handle does not). A hand brake is another desirable feature to enable to slow or stop the launch at will. When launching is done on a steep ramp, the advantages of a winch brake becomes readily apparent.

POWER WINCHES

Electric power winches take most of the labor out of retrieving the boat to the trailer, and are

ELECTRIC POWER WINCH

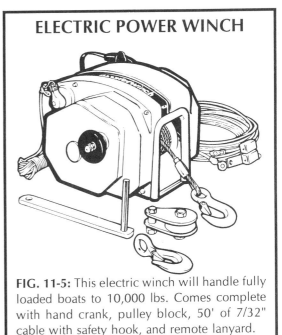

FIG. 11-5: This electric winch will handle fully loaded boats to 10,000 lbs. Comes complete with hand crank, pulley block, 50' of 7/32" cable with safety hook, and remote lanyard.

Courtesy POWERWINCH

how to build boat trailers

especially advantageous when launching heavy boats on steep ramps. Available in varying sizes and capacities, the electric winch operates off of the towing vehicle battery. Particularly for larger craft where retrieving the boat by hand is quite a chore, the power winch is indeed a pleasure to have. The electric power winch is only as efficient as the power it draws. The wiring is through a heavy duty wiring harness, circuit breaker, and switch usually furnished with the winch. Electric winches under full load typically require about 80 amps from the 12 volt battery; thus, heavy wires are required to the battery of the towing vehicle. It's usually advisable to run the tow vehicle motor at an idle when using the electric power winch to assure a constant power source. A remote control feature is desirable so the winch can be controlled from some distance.   ❖

LIGHTS

Unfortunately, boat trailer lighting requirements vary considerably from state to state; uniformity is being discussed but, as yet, is not a reality. Before starting to think of wiring the lights for a boat trailer, check the appropriate department of your state for their requirements. Nothing in this text should be considered to be the last word, and the suggestions noted should not be substituted for the legal requirements of a given state.

Boat trailer lights lead a rough life. They're expected to be reliable at all times even though their conditions of use are conducive to a short life and trouble. A trailer light becomes heated while traveling and when submerged in cold water during the launch, tend to blow out. The constant immersion in water sooner or later tend to take a toll on lights, plugs, and wires and cause a malfunction.

A boat trailer that is to be submerged during launching and retrieval has several options to prevent lighting failure. The most obvious solution is to keep the lights out of the water. If the trailer is to be submerged, lights can be mounted on a bar or bumper that can be removed prior to launching (See Chapter 10, "Tie Downs"). Light bars at the transom will take care of the tail, brake and directional signals and clearance lights can be mounted atop guide bars or made removable.

The use of special waterproof boat trailer lights will help, however, some are not completely waterproof. They are, however, far superior to recreational trailer or automotive type lights that will cause trouble immediately if submerged.

TRAILER WIRING FOR LIGHTS

The trailer wiring must be a stranded type, heavily insulated, and of proper gage (AWG) to carry the combined lighting load. Usually 16 gage is satisfactory for trailer lighting circuits with a minimum of 14 gage for electric brakes. The thicker the wire and insulation the better. A separately jacketed wire with several integral leads is preferable to prevent breaking, chafing and shorting out. Use only stranded copper wire; single strand "AC house" wire should not be used. Wiring harnesses are commercially available to connect the trailer lights to the towing vehicle. They are color coded and come with trailer to towing vehicle connectors. Get the heavy duty marine type and save a lot of future trouble.

A typical 12 volt DC (direct current) towing vehicle electrical system has the battery grounded to the frame or body. Trailer lighting systems are similar; the ground lead from the towing vehicle is usually connected to the trailer frame. However, some prefer a separate ground wire run to and securely fastened to each light, it's mounting lug, or ground lead.

how to build boat trailers

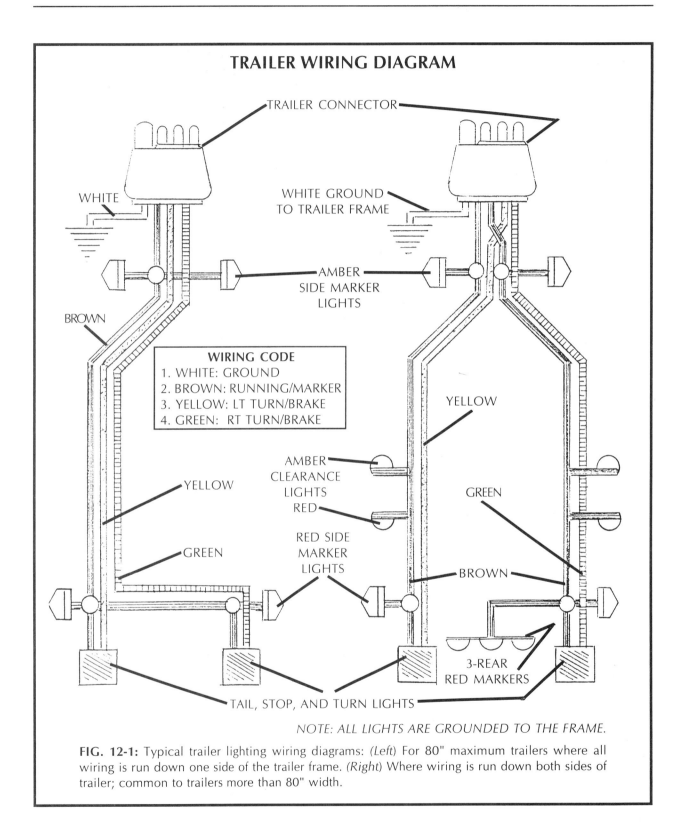

TRAILER WIRING DIAGRAM

TRAILER CONNECTOR

WHITE GROUND
TO TRAILER FRAME

WHITE

AMBER
SIDE MARKER
LIGHTS

BROWN

WIRING CODE
1. WHITE: GROUND
2. BROWN: RUNNING/MARKER
3. YELLOW: LT TURN/BRAKE
4. GREEN: RT TURN/BRAKE

YELLOW

YELLOW

AMBER
CLEARANCE
LIGHTS
RED

GREEN

GREEN

RED SIDE
MARKER
LIGHTS

BROWN

3-REAR
RED MARKERS

TAIL, STOP, AND TURN LIGHTS

NOTE: ALL LIGHTS ARE GROUNDED TO THE FRAME.

FIG. 12-1: Typical trailer lighting wiring diagrams: (*Left*) For 80" maximum trailers where all wiring is run down one side of the trailer frame. (*Right*) Where wiring is run down both sides of trailer; common to trailers more than 80" width.

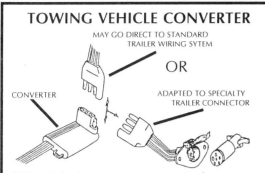

TOWING VEHICLE CONVERTER

MAY GO DIRECT TO STANDARD
TRAILER WIRING SYTEM

OR

CONVERTER

ADAPTED TO SPECIALTY
TRAILER CONNECTOR

FIG. 12-2: A converter is required to accommodate standard trailer lighting to that of foreign and some American tow vehicles that have separate hot wires for the brake and turn signal. Courtesy TAP

The importance of a positive connection between the ground wire or frames of the towing vehicle and the trailer cannot be over emphasized. More trailer light failures are attributed to a poor ground connection than any other one factor. Depending on the connection of the coupler to the ball hitch to act as a ground often results in poor contact and leads to flickering trailer lights. Make the ground connection from the towing vehicle to the trailer a positive junction by using bolts or other methods to make metal to metal contact. If the lights do not make contact with the trailer frame, such as with removable light bars, a separate ground must be used.

A ground and positive wire activates the trailer lights. The typical light fitting is grounded to the trailer frame by a mounting lug; a separate ground wire is required when lights do not mount to the trailer frame. Each grounded trailer light has one hot wire that fastens to the corresponding light on the trailer. However, a stop/turn signal light may have two filaments that require two hot leads plus the ground. Such a system is typical of many towing ve-

hicles; one filament is activated for illuminating the tail light while the second filament (thus brighter light) is activated for the turn signals. Foreign and some American cars use a separate turn (usually amber) signal and red brake light in lieu of the dual filament method and thus require a separate connection to each light. The wiring diagram shown in FIG. 12-1 is intended for the dual filament brake/turn signal and will not operate off of a towing vehicle that does not use the same method. However, a special converter can be obtained to convert a towing vehicle DC system with separate turn and brake light wiring, and use the trailer wiring method shown in FIG. 12-1. A typical converter and connector are shown in FIG. 12-2.

Secure permanent trailer lighting wires to the frame so it can't chafe against a sharp corner or edge. All wiring should be supported at close intervals and located to afford protection from road splash, stones, abrasion, grease, oil, and fuel. Run the wires inside tubular trailer frames or the inside corner of structural steel members when possible.

The accepted color coding for boat trailer wiring is:

WHITE = ground
BROWN = clearance and side marker lights.
YELLOW = left turn and stop light.
GREEN = right turn and stop light.

Wire connections should be positive; don't use common wire nuts. Use special DC plastic clamps with the wire twisted together before clamping, or crimp type connectors preferably with open ends sealed with waterproofing sealant. One of the best junctions is made by spreading the ends of the stranded wires to be

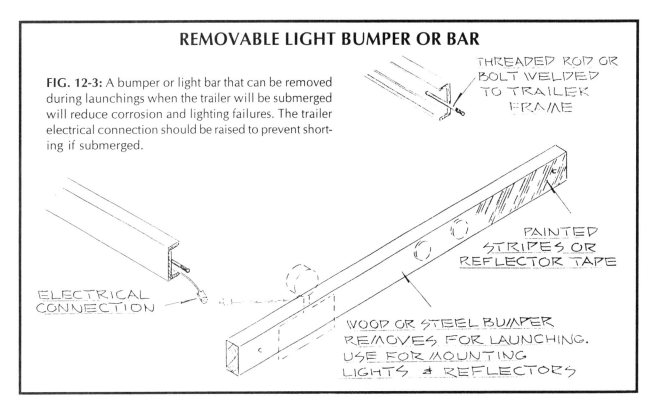

REMOVABLE LIGHT BUMPER OR BAR

FIG. 12-3: A bumper or light bar that can be removed during launchings when the trailer will be submerged will reduce corrosion and lighting failures. The trailer electrical connection should be raised to prevent shorting if submerged.

THREADED ROD OR BOLT WELDED TO TRAILER FRAME

PAINTED STRIPES OR REFLECTOR TAPE

ELECTRICAL CONNECTION

WOOD OR STEEL BUMPER REMOVES FOR LAUNCHING. USE FOR MOUNTING LIGHTS & REFLECTORS

joined and twisting them alternately over one another and then soldered together. Wrap the junction with at least two layers of waterproof tape; optionally, follow with a waterproof sealant coating for extra protection.

From a practical and safety standpoint, all trailers should be equipped with at least the minimum lighting used on the rear of the typical automobile; stop lights, directional turn signals, license, and tail lights. Rear reflectors should also be used on the right and left sides and may be incorporated in the lights if permitted by state law. Clearance lights and/or reflectors are desirable and may also be required. Right and left rear lights for stop, turn, and tail lights should be located as far apart as practical and positioned so that they are plainly visible when viewed from the driver's seat of a following vehicle. Tail light heights are generally a minimum of 15" above the road and 72" maximum.

WIRING METHODS

Two types of trailer wiring methods shown in FIG. 12 -1 are common and accepted as standard. One method runs the brown (clearance and side marker lights) wire down each side of the frame while the other runs all wires down one side of the frame and across the rear. Either is acceptable. The "all wires down one side" wiring method is typical of trailers under 80" in width. Although side marker lights may not be required, they are recommended. The wiring system using wires down both sides of the trailer frame, shown on the right side of FIG. 12-1, is typical of trailers over 80" in width where additional clearance and three red rear light markers are required.

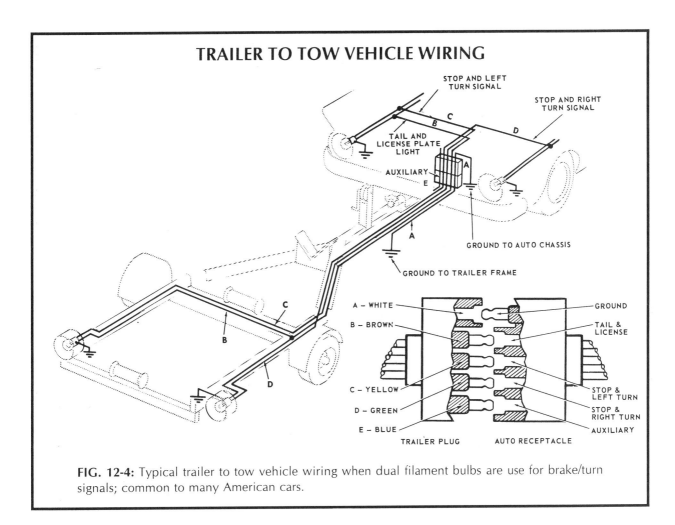

TRAILER TO TOW VEHICLE WIRING

FIG. 12-4: Typical trailer to tow vehicle wiring when dual filament bulbs are use for brake/turn signals; common to many American cars.

TOW VEHICLE LIGHTING CONNECTOR

The towing vehicle wiring is coupled to the trailer through a special male and female connector. Usually made of molded rubber or plastic, the trailer end has a female opening for the ground and male projections for the balance of the wires. Connectors are in pairs; one part for the trailer and the matching half for the towing vehicle. Other connectors may have receptacles similar to the convenience outlet in a house: a male and female mating connector. Unfortunately, connectors are not standard and one from company "A" will probably not mate to one made by company "B". A typical connector used on boat trailers will accommodate four wires although multiple prong types are available to connect auxiliary wiring such as electric brakes.

The trailer connector is located near the trailer coupler with the wires long enough to reach the towing vehicle receptacle. The trailer wiring should be slack enough to compensate for sharp turns and still have adequate clearance from the ground. Disconnect the trailer from the towing vehicle during wet launching and

how to build boat trailers

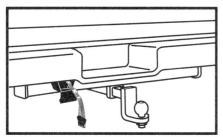  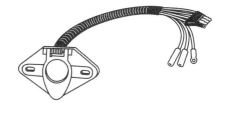
loop it over the winch stand so it won't get wet or damaged by the launching or retrieval procedure.

The towing vehicle half of the connector can be carried in the trunk of a car. However, a wire harness caddie with cover, shown in FIG. 12-5, anchored to the vehicle eliminates pinching the wire when the trunk lid or van door is closed. Other types utilize a female receptacle with spring cover mounted on the towing vehicle; a matching male plug with wires attached completes the connection to the trailer. Towing vehicle connectors with waterproof covers or caps to protect the receptacle from the elements when not in use are recommended.

It is probable that the towing vehicle flasher that activates the trailer directional signal light will not stand the additional load unless it has a special "towing package". If normal operation of the directional indicators does not occur with the trailer lights connected, the flasher unit should be replaced with a heavy-duty unit. Heavy-duty flashers are available at auto parts stores throughout the country.   ❖

HITCHES

The trailer hitch is one of the most important links in the chain of equipment that makes for successful trailer boating. For such a seemingly simple piece of equipment, the job it has to do is complex. When the towing vehicle accelerates, a tremendous tension is set up, tending to separate it from the trailer. Conversely, when the vehicle is stopping, a compression thrust tries to push the trailer forward. The weight of the trailer tongue on the hitch tends to force the rear of the towing vehicle down and throw the trailer out of towing alignment. This compresses the soft car springs intended to give the passengers an easy ride beyond their normal range.

Many passenger automobiles are not recommended for trailer towing, and those that are usually have limited towing capabilities. Some vehicle manufacturers have a limitation on the gross combined weight of the towing vehicle and that of the loaded trailer and/or tongue weight. Vans and utility sport vehicles generally have higher ratings than passenger cars and are capable of carrying larger boats. A towing limitation of 2000 lbs. would enable the vehicle to tow an open powerboat of about 17', a 15' cruising powerboat, or a centerboard (unballasted) 16' sailboat. The foregoing figures are estimates and are intended to give an approximate idea of what size boats can be towed with the typical passenger vehicle rated for towing. Check the actual weight of your boat with all gear on board plus the trailer weight and compare it to the towing vehicle's capabilities.

TRAILER WEIGHTS				
Trailer	No.	Trailer Size		
Capacity	Axles	Length	Width	Wt.
1000 lbs.	1	15'4"	62"	295 lbs.
1500 lbs.	1	15'4"	62"	305 lbs.
2000 lbs	1	17'2"	88"	492 lbs.
2450 lbs.	1	18'2"	96"	522 lbs.
2999 lbs.	1	18'2"	96"	625 lbs.
3500 lbs.	1	19'8"	96"	677 lbs.
5000 lbs.	2	20'8"	96"	933 lbs.
7000 lbs.	2	27'9"	96"	1512 lbs.

Use this chart to approximate the weight of a typical boat trailer.

Use a vehicle that's suited to the task of towing the loaded boat and trailer weight. Determine this not by what a salesperson states; check directly to the source, either the owners manual or manufacturers written specifications. If you're purchasing a new vehicle, obtain the special trailer towing option package. A trailer towing package will vary from make to make; a few changes and/or additions are listed in the following. Higher ratio axle gearing (axle ratio), special trailer towing suspension, factory installed trailer hitch and trailer wiring harness, special power steering fluid cooler, and a myriad of heavy duty items such as radiator, transmission, turning signal flasher, engine oil cooler, brakes, tires, and alternator are used to properly equip the vehicle for towing.

How To Build Boat Trailers

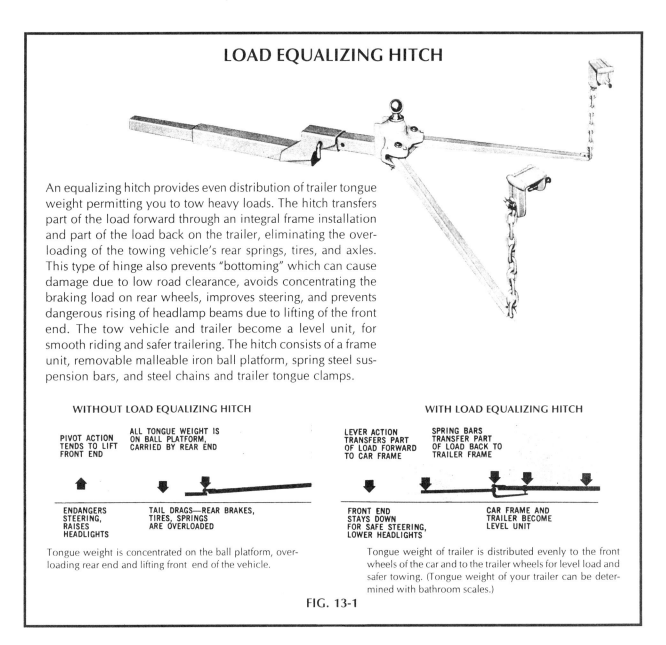

LOAD EQUALIZING HITCH

An equalizing hitch provides even distribution of trailer tongue weight permitting you to tow heavy loads. The hitch transfers part of the load forward through an integral frame installation and part of the load back on the trailer, eliminating the overloading of the towing vehicle's rear springs, tires, and axles. This type of hinge also prevents "bottoming" which can cause damage due to low road clearance, avoids concentrating the braking load on rear wheels, improves steering, and prevents dangerous rising of headlamp beams due to lifting of the front end. The tow vehicle and trailer become a level unit, for smooth riding and safer trailering. The hitch consists of a frame unit, removable malleable iron ball platform, spring steel suspension bars, and steel chains and trailer tongue clamps.

WITHOUT LOAD EQUALIZING HITCH

PIVOT ACTION TENDS TO LIFT FRONT END

ALL TONGUE WEIGHT IS ON BALL PLATFORM, CARRIED BY REAR END

ENDANGERS STEERING, RAISES HEADLIGHTS

TAIL DRAGS—REAR BRAKES, TIRES, SPRINGS ARE OVERLOADED

Tongue weight is concentrated on the ball platform, overloading rear end and lifting front end of the vehicle.

WITH LOAD EQUALIZING HITCH

LEVER ACTION TRANSFERS PART OF LOAD FORWARD TO CAR FRAME

SPRING BARS TRANSFERS PART OF LOAD BACK TO TRAILER FRAME

FRONT END STAYS DOWN FOR SAFE STEERING, LOWER HEADLIGHTS

CAR FRAME AND TRAILER BECOME LEVEL UNIT

Tongue weight of trailer is distributed evenly to the front wheels of the car and to the trailer wheels for level load and safer towing. (Tongue weight of your trailer can be determined with bathroom scales.)

FIG. 13-1

TRAILER HITCH TYPES

The three basic types of trailer hitches for the towing vehicle are: bumper hitch, frame hitch (both weight carrying hitches), and weight distribution hitch (sometimes called equalizing hitch).

The bumper hitch (weight carrying) is technically defined as a mechanical or structural device that bolts, or is otherwise fastened, to the towing vehicle. No connection is made to the frame or other structural member. In the past, such hitches were commonly used as they were inexpensive, easy to install, and worked well for light load trailering. Current automotive

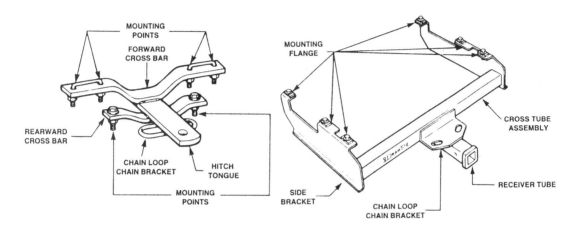

FRAME HITCH

(WEIGHT CARRYING HITCHES)

FIXED-PLATFORM HITCH   RECEIVER (used with drawbar ball mount)

FIG 13-2: *(Left)* A fixed-platform hitch is a complete integral assembly. *(Right)* A receiver hitch shown with the drawbar or ball mount removed.   Courtesy DRAW-TITE, INC.

bumpers are built to absorb collision shocks but not the stresses required for safe trailering. Some states do not allow bumper hitches, and using them will probably void your auto warranty. Pickup truck hitches mounted on a centerline step are classed as "step hitches", and are not considered to be bumper hitches. Step hitches sometimes have comparatively low towing capacity, however, heavy duty units are available to increase the capacity. (See FIG. 13-3.)

FRAME HITCH

A frame hitch (weight carrying) is a mechanical and/or structural device that fastens or bolts to the towing vehicle's structural members,

which can include the frame or unitized body. Such a hitch provides a solid connection to the rear end of the towing vehicle. It does not, however, transfer any of the hitch weight to anywhere but the rear of the towing vehicle. Today this is the most common hitch used to couple the average size boat trailer to the towing vehicle. Bolt on hitch packages are available for almost any car rated for towing. Install a hitch that is strong enough to match or exceed the towing vehicles capacity.

FIFTH WHEEL HITCHES

Fifth wheel hitches are not common for coupling boat trailers to their towing vehicle. However, they enable more of a load to be carried

How To Build Boat Trailers

than practical with most other hitches. Fifth wheel hitches are used with pickup trucks and are mounted on the truck bed just forward of the rear wheels. This shifts the tongue weight forward to a location that more equally distributes the load to all four wheels of the towing vehicle. The hitch is cumbersome and impractical for most trailer boats that will be frequently launched over a ramp. However, when towing a boat and trailer with a gross weight of over 10,000 lbs., a fifth wheel hitch is a practical solution.

LOAD EQUALIZING HITCH

A weight distribution or load equalizing hitch is a mechanical device that connects the trailer to the towing vehicle. By means of spring action leverage on both the trailer and vehicle

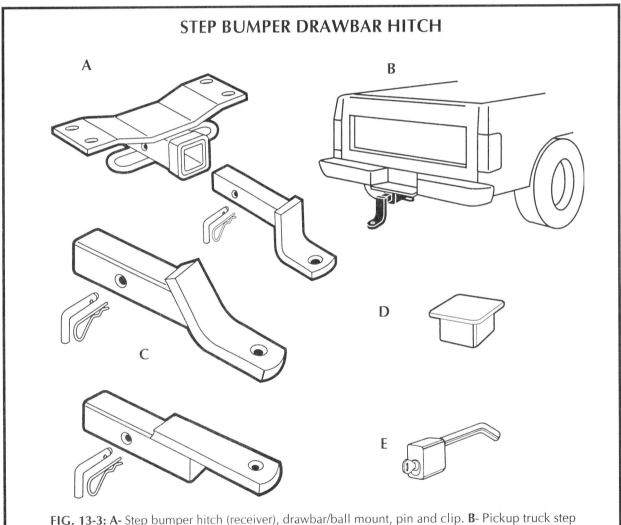

STEP BUMPER DRAWBAR HITCH

A   B   C   D   E

FIG. 13-3: A- Step bumper hitch (receiver), drawbar/ball mount, pin and clip. **B-** Pickup truck step bumper hitch with ball mount. **C-** Optional drawbar/ball mounts that alter the height of the ball. **D-** Receiver cover enhances the appearance when the drawbar is removed. **E-** Locking pin to prevent drawbar theft. *Courtesy FULTON PERFORMANCE PRODUCTS*

frames, it distributes the imposed vertical load at the hitch and coupling connection equally on the wheels of the towing vehicle and trailer. The towing vehicle thus loaded stays level with the road. This type of hitch virtually eliminates all possibility of sway, oscillation, and roll. Steering is better, stability is improved, and the rear end sag at the trailer to towing vehicle connection is eliminated. A weight-distributing system includes a receiver attached to the tow vehicle, a removable hitch head and spring bar assembly that fits in the receiver opening, and hook-up brackets that connect the spring bars to the trailer frame. See FIG. 13-1.

Some authorities feel that weight equalizing hitches are required only when loads exceed 4000 lbs., most U.S. manufacturers say that such a hitch is required for anything over 2000 lbs., while some foreign auto builders don't recommend their use at all. A trailer equipped with surge brakes may be partially or totally inactivated when using a load equalizer hitch; check with the hitch people before considering such a combination. Most people who use weight equalizing hitches, particularly with heavier loads, are enthusiastic with the results and wouldn't trail a boat without such a device.

BALL HITCHES

Ball hitches utilize two basic types of ball mounts, fixed and drawbar. A ball that is located atop a platform extension of the hitch, is called a fixed type. The typical drawbar hitch

---

BALLS

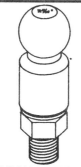

HIGH LIFT BALL

TYPICAL STANDARD BALL

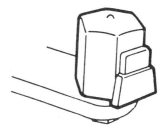

PROTECTIVE BALL COVER

A "Ball" is the spherically shaped member with a neck and seat. The seat rests upon a hitch platform. A threaded portion below the seat extends through the hitch platform and is fastened to it with a lock washer and nut.
Balls are classified by relating the diameter of the ball to a specific Trailer Classification.

Trailer Classification	Ball Diameter
Class 1	1 7/8"
Class 2	2"
Class 3	2"
Class 4	2 5/16"

There are many types of balls on the market. Some are made in one piece, others are made in two or more pieces (a bolt extends down from the center of the ball). They are also made in various heights an shapes. Most balls are identified on the top with the ball diameter such as 1 7/8", 2", etc. The ball should be used with the Trailer Classification as described above.

FIG. 13-4

SAFETY CHAINS

"Safety chains" are the flexible tension members connected from the front portion of the towed vehicle to the rear portion of the towing vehicle. Their purpose is to retain connection between towed and towing vehicle in the event of failure of the ball, socket, coupler, or hitch.

TRAILER CLASSIFICATION	CHAIN SPECIFICATIONS	APPROX DIAM. OF STEEL IN LINK
CLass 1	Steel Welded Chain or equivalent in strength - 2000 lbs. miminum breaking test load.	3/16"
Class 2	Steel Welded Chain or equivalent in strength - 3500 lbs minimum breaking test load.	1/4"
Class 3	Steel Welded Chain or equivalent in strength - 5000 lbs. minimum breaking test load.	5/16"
Class 4	The strength rating of each length of safety chain shall be equal in minimum break test load to the gross weight of the trailer including its respective load.	3/8" to 7/16"

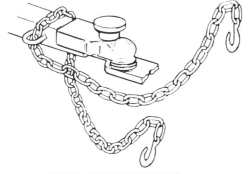

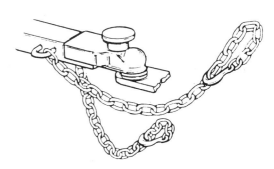

TYPICAL SINGLE SAFETY CHAIN INSTALLATION

TYPICAL DOUBLE SAFETY CHAIN INSTALLATION

Safety chains must be connected to the front of the trailer or tongue, *not* to the coupler, by bolts or other devices. The minimum strength of these devices, including those which attach to the towing vehicle, must be equal to the Maximum Gross Trailer Weight. No welding, torching, or machining operation shall be performed on the chain by the installer or the operator to attach it to the trailer.

Review the illustrations, "Typical Single Safety Chain Installation" and "Typical Double Safety Chain Installation". Both the single and double chains must be crossed *under* the tongue. They must be oriented in such a manner as to prevent the tongue from dropping to the ground in the event of failure to the hitch, coupler, or ball. The chains must be connected to the towing vehicle so that the slack for each length of chain between the trailer and the towing vehicle is the same, and must have no more slack when in use than is necessary to permit proper turning of the vehicles. The forward end of the chain must be attached to the towing vehicle, *not* to the ball, but to the hitch or other frame member. The chain must be looped around the member and hooked back into itself.

FIG. 13-5

consists of a receiver tube which attaches to the vehicle frame or pickup step bumper, a removable drawbar/ball mount, ball, and drawbar locking pin. A drawbar ball mount has several advantages. A rectangular tube or receiver extends, or is part of, the trailer hitch. The ball with drawbar mount slides inside the receiver and can be removed when not in use thus eliminating blocking the license plate, rust due to exposure, and possible theft. See FIG. 13-3 A.

The ball hitch should be located so that the trailer chassis is level when coupled to the towing vehicle. This is easily done by blocking the trailer level and measuring the height from the ground to the inside of the coupler. This di-

mension should be equal to the height from the ground to the top of the ball assembly as it mounts to the hitch. It may be possible to adjust the hitch height of the towing vehicle so the trailer is level by using a standard or a high lift ball or couplers that attach above or below the trailer frame level. An "L" shaped drawbar can also be used to adjust the hitch ball height. See FIGS. 13-3B and 13-4.

The ball hitch must be located on the centerline of the towing vehicle and securely fastened to the frame or step bumper. The shank of the ball should fit securely into the hole in the ball mount, and a lock washer used between the mount and the ball nut, thoroughly tightened

---

HITCHES

Definition: A hitch generally means that part of the primary connecting system normally mounted on the towing vehicle. This includes a ball support platform upon which a ball is mounted for connecting the trailer. There are two basic types of hiches:

1. WCH - "Weight Carrying Hitch" is a mechanical and/or structural device which connects the trailer to the towing vehicle but is not designed to distribute the tongue load; it carries the full tongue load at the ball connection.
2. WDH - "Weight Distributing Hitch" is a mechanical device which connects the trailer to the towing vehicle and by means of leverage, the load is distributed from the trailer tongue to *all* towing vehicle *and* trailer wheels.

Classification: Hitches are classified in accordance with the maximum recommended tongue load based upon trailer classification.

Maximum Recommended Tongue Weights by Trailer Classification

Class Trailer	Maximum Gross Tailer Weight (MGTW), lbs.*	Maximum Static Tongue Loads, in lbs.**	Recommended Type of Hitch
1	2,000 lbs. or less	200 300	Weight carrying hitch Weight distrib. hitch
2	2,001 thru 3,500 lbs.	300 500	Weight carrying hitch Weight disttrib. hitch
3	3,501 thru 5,000 lbs.	15% MGTW*	Weight ditrib. hitch
4	5,001 thru 10,000 lbs.	15% MGTW*	Weight distrib. hitch

*   Maximum Gross Trailer Weight
**   Maximum load at the ball when vehicle is at rest.
    Minimum load at the ball for good towability is 10% of MGTW.

FIG. 13-6

and checked each time the trailer is towed. Be sure that the ball hitch does not obstruct the view of the license plate when not towing a trailer; state laws require that the license plate of the towing vehicle be visible at all times. If the ball obscures the plate, a receiver with drawbar is advisable.

Lubricate the trailer ball and inside the coupler prior to connecting to the towing vehicle. When the trailer is not being used, the ball should be covered with a plastic or metal protector, available from many manufacturers, or a split tennis ball forced over the ball hitch.

SAFETY CHAINS

All trailers must have a safety chain coupled between the chassis of the towing vehicle and the frame of the trailer. The chain should be welded steel or of a type equivalent in strength, with a minimum capacity in a break test load equal to the gross weight of the trailer including its load. Safety chains should not be attached to any part of the ball or to fastenings common to the ball. No welding should be performed on the chain subsequent to that of its manufacture. Safety chains should be connected on opposite sides of the trailer tongue or frame, crossed under the tongue, and connected to the towing vehicle in a manner which prevents the tongue from dropping to the ground, and which maintains directional control in the event of coupling failure. The chain should have no more slack than is necessary to permit proper turning of the vehicles. Eyes provided on the hitch platform are considered a part of the towing vehicle for the purpose of attaching safety chains. See FIG. 13-5.

TRAILER TONGUE WEIGHT

What weight should be carried on the hitch of the towing vehicle? A correctly balanced trailer will carry most of the weight on the axle or axles and yet have enough tongue weight to track properly. In past years about 5% of the total weight of the boat, trailer, and gear was carried at the tongue when such total weight did not exceed 1500 pounds. Heavier trailers might carry 7%-8% of the total weight for tongue load. Current practice dictates a minimum of 10% of the maximum gross trailer weight be carried at the hitch. FIG. 13-6 gives recommendations for loads on the towing vehicle for various types of hitches.

The amount of weight on the hitch can be readily determined by using bathroom scales under the coupler when the trailer is sitting level. When tongue weight exceeds the bathroom scales capacity, block the trailer wheels fore and aft with the trailer on a level firm surface. See FIG.13-7. Use a jack and raise the tongue until the trailer is level. Place blocking equal to the bathroom scale height, in line with and 1' outboard of the coupler centerline. Center the bathroom scale 2' on the other side of the coupler centerline. Lay a short length of pipe or rod atop the blocking and bathroom scale and adjust these so the 1' and 2' spacing from the coupler centerline is accurate. Place a 4" x 4" (any wood or metal beam that will support the weight can be used) atop the two pipes and use a strong support from the beam to the tongue, adjusting the height so the trailer is level. Before the trailer is lowered on the support, re-calibrate the bathroom scale to read "0". Lower the tongue so the trailer is level when resting on the support. The tongue

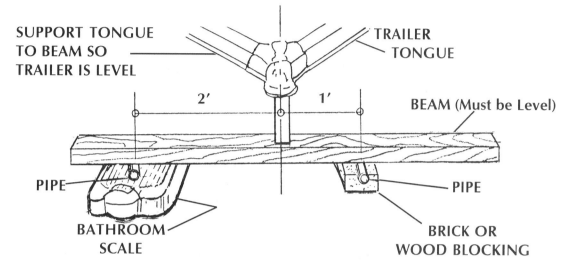

METHOD FOR MEASURING TONGUE WEIGHT

SUPPORT TONGUE
TO BEAM SO
TRAILER IS LEVEL

TRAILER
TONGUE

2'   1'

BEAM (Must be Level)

PIPE

PIPE

BATHROOM
SCALE

BRICK OR
WOOD BLOCKING

FORMULA:
TONGUE WEIGHT = 3 X WEIGHT REGISTERED ON THE SCALE

FIG. 13-7: When tongue weight exceeds scale capacity, use the above method but respace the 2' dimension to 3' and replace the "3" in the formula with "4". For complete accuracy, "zero" bathroom scale with beam in place prior to reading weight.

weight is found by multiplying the bathroom scale reading by three.

Tongue weight can be altered by moving the boat forward or aft, or by shifting the axle position when the undercarriage is mounted on a movable bracket as shown in Chapter 3. ❖

BOAT LAUNCHING & RETRIEVING

Have you ever gone to a launching area and watched people launch their boats from a trailer? If you have, you will marvel at the efficiency of some and possibly double over with laughter at the pathetic attempts of others. It should be added, however, that in most instances it isn't the individual that is at fault. If the rig, trailer and boat are not properly mated with winch, proper guides, and other appendages, even the most experienced individual will make a mess out of what is a relatively easy job. With a little observation and thought, most trailer launchings can be simplified.

UPRIGHT GUIDES

How should the trailer be equipped for easy launching and retrieving at a typical launch ramp? Probably the most important thing is to have guides on the trailer to keep the boat from drifting to one side. Preferably these upright guides are located near the transom of the boat and spaced wide enough apart to clear the maximum beam of the boat. They should, however, taper down so that as the boat floats down, it is properly positioned on the trailer. Why struggle to center the aft end of the boat on the trailer? If you have no guides, it means getting in the water to hold the boat from drifting. If guides are not used or improperly placed, a lot of muscle will be required to center the boat on the trailer after it's pulled up on dry land. It is desirable to have the guides high enough so they are readily visible and won't be submerged when launching, and preferably roller equipped and well padded. They should also be stout enough to withstand the weight of the boat drifting or being blown against them. Upright guides may also be used as supports for an athwartship hold down, a light bar to hold the lights and license plate, or as an aft form to sup-

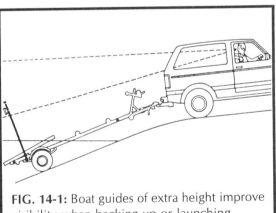

FIG. 14-1: Boat guides of extra height improve visibility when backing up or launching.

port a sailboat mast as described in Chapter 10, "Tie Downs".

Upright guides in the midsection of the boat and also at the bow are advantageous when launching or retrieving a boat when the site is subject to winds or wave action. With a series of uprights, a rope can be used to form a triangular area around

FIG. 14-2: These vertical uprights, located near the transom, are padded with tubular boat fenders to prevent marring the boat. Commercially available uprights may incorporate roller guides and provisions for lights.

the trailer with the apex at the bow. This line will prevent the boat from drifting, and with proper guides, the boat will settle in the cradle. In lieu of the rope, these upright guides can be connected with well padded pipe or rod. Although rather unusual in appearance, the retrieval of the boat to the trailer will be greatly simplified.

A winch on the trailer tongue is preferable for most launching conditions, along with a bow form to firmly hold the bow of the boat. A bow form must keep the boat from going forward, aft, or to either side when on the trailer. Although rope can be used, a positive method of locking the boat to the stem as shown in Chapter 10 is preferable.

PREPARING TO LAUNCH

Although elementary, always check the launching area. If it is a nice paved ramp, launching should be quick and easy. However, if others are launching at one certain area of the ramp, a good second look is in order. Perhaps the launch ramp drops off or ends quickly in the unused areas. During the launch, you are liable to find the boat floating quickly, but the trailer may be long gone to the bottom of the lake. Perhaps the unused launch area is silted over and the trailer will go just so far and get stuck. Ask other launchers why an area is unused. If no one is using the launching site, check with care. As stated, this is elementary, but many who have trailered a boat to different launch sites for a few years have at one time or other been in an embarrassing situation caused by launching without a thorough check of the ramp site.

Prepare for the launch prior to getting on the ramp, particularly if others are waiting. Put the boat's transom drain plugs in place and remove the tie-downs. Disconnect the trailer lights and be sure the connectors are secured so as not to contact the water. Tighten the winch and connect a rope to the boat that will be readily available when the boat floats free. Be sure everything is ready; start the outboard or inboard motor and immediately shut if off. Just make sure it will start and run when in the water. Tilt the outboard or outdrive so it won't bottom out during the launch. Raise the mast and rig a sailboat away from the ramp as long as their are no overhead obstructions on the way to the launch site. Describe the launching procedure to guests or friends who are new to trailer boating; explain what they are to do if their help is required.

how to build boat trailers

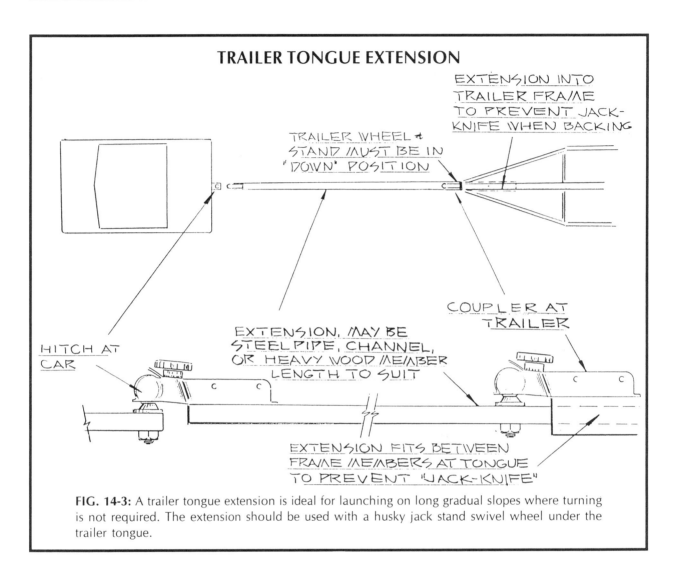

TRAILER TONGUE EXTENSION

EXTENSION INTO TRAILER FRAME TO PREVENT JACK-KNIFE WHEN BACKING

TRAILER WHEEL & STAND MUST BE IN "DOWN" POSITION

COUPLER AT TRAILER

HITCH AT CAR

EXTENSION, MAY BE STEEL PIPE, CHANNEL, OR HEAVY WOOD MEMBER LENGTH TO SUIT

EXTENSION FITS BETWEEN FRAME MEMBERS AT TONGUE TO PREVENT "JACK-KNIFE"

FIG. 14-3: A trailer tongue extension is ideal for launching on long gradual slopes where turning is not required. The extension should be used with a husky jack stand swivel wheel under the trailer tongue.

RAMP LAUNCHING

Back down the ramp slowly; don't get closer to the water than necessary. Keep the tow vehicle wheels and tailpipe clear of the water, consider waves or back wash that may sweep up the ramp. Back down the ramp far enough so the boat will roll off the trailer into the water without undue effort. Set the brakes on the towing vehicle; chocks may be considered on steep ramps. Release the winch line coupling the boat to the trailer slowly. When the boat starts to float, disconnect the winch line, grab the bow line attached to the boat, and push the boat free of the trailer. Secure the boat to a nearby dock or hold it off the beach while the tow vehicle and trailer go to the parking area.

Retrieval is similar but in reverse. Back the trailer in place and connect the winch line to the boat. Slowly winch the boat over the rollers and bunks until the bow form mates solidly. A steep ramp makes for an easy launch, but retrieval can be a problem, particularly when the ramp is wet or algae covered. What may be a great ramp when the tide is in, may be slippery when the tide is out. Reducing the towing vehicles tire pressure and/or adding weight to the driving wheels will help. Start the retrieval slowly; avoid spinning the wheels. Clear the ramp and prepare the rig for the road; check lights, tie-downs, safety chains, etc., and you're on your way.

It may become impossible to retrieve a fixed keel sailboat when the tide is out. If trailering this type of boat, you should be aware of the condition of the ramp when the tide is out, to avoid having to wait for a turn in the tide before the boat can be retrieved. And of course, it would be helpful to know when the tide will be out. This information is usually printed in area newspapers.

BEACH LAUNCHING

Paved launching ramps are a boater's dream and are common, but launching through a sandy beach or an unpaved natural bottom is sometimes necessary. The first requisite is a rope, cable, or chain. The size will be governed by the load, but don't skimp. The writer uses a 3/4" rope 100' in length for retrieving boats and trailers to the 18' size. The length may seem long, but it is imperative that the towing vehicle be on solid ground, particularly when retrieving from sand beaches or tidal waters. Assuming that the launching place has been inspected, the boat, trailer, and towing vehicle should be backed as close as practical to the water's edge with the towing vehicle's drive wheels on solid ground. Unload all the extra gear carried in the boat and remove any hold downs; take off the lights, if they are sepa-

rate, and disconnect the trailer from the towing vehicle. If on a steep slope, be sure you chock the wheels of the trailer before disconnecting the rig. Lower the bow wheel, if you have one, and fasten a rope, cable, or chain from the towing vehicle trailer hitch to the trailer. If launching over loose sand, it may not be practical to use the bow wheel. In this type of launch, a skid under the tongue may be more practical.

Don't make the fastening to the trailer or towing vehicle a major project. When using a rope, make an eye on either end and loop one eye over the trailer hitch. Take the other eye back around the trailer frame and loop it over the trailer coupler. If you are using cable or chain, do the same or use hooks or eyes for quick release. Fasten a rope to the boat and keep a loose coil in hand during the launching.

When all is set, remove the chocks and start the boat going down the incline. When launching through sand or loose dirt, get the rig going FAST (everyone pushes) so it won't get stuck. Just as you get to the point that the boat starts to float, give the boat a strong push, holding to the line attached to the bow of the boat. With the proper guides and rollers, the boat will float out of the trailer easily and simply. Bring the boat to the beach or secure it; then use the towing vehicle, with line attached, to pull the trailer out of the water. Why people break their backs pulling and tugging when the car or towing truck can do the job is a mystery. When the trailer is high and dry on solid ground, put chocks behind the trailer wheels (if required), remove the line, couple the trailer, and you are off to the parking area.

TIDAL BEACH RETRIEVAL

(Left) When retrieving or launching a boat in tidal conditions, a long rope from towing vehicle to the trailer tongue is a necessity. The boat retrieval, in this instance, was through a sandy tidal beach with a very gentle slope.

(Right) The trailer is rolled into the water and the boat pushed beyond the partially submerged trailer uprights.

(Left) The launching site slope is very gradual requiring the trailer wheels to be well submerged to enable the boat to be winched onto the trailer. (Below) The boat and trailer are pulled over the tidal beach by a rope from the towing vehicle to the trailer tongue.

FIG. 14-4

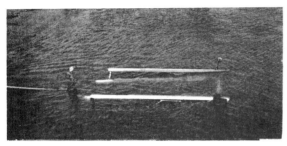

FIG. 14-5: (*Above*) This trailer, equipped with a tongue extension, has been completely submerged. The longitudinal guides keep the boat centered on the trailer while the boat powers the trailer toward the beach.
(*Left*) A longitudinal catwalk along the trailer keeps this individual from getting wet when connecting the winch line to the boat.

The retrieval of the boat is similar. Again, fasten the line from the car to the trailer and push the trailer out deep enough to accommodate the boat. Hold the bow line of the boat and give the boat a stiff shove well beyond the trailer. Use the bow line or winch rope to pull the trailer through the upright guides and lift the trailer tongue to fit the boat securely into the bow form. After securing the boat to the trailer, pull it out with the rope attached to the towing vehicle. Follow through as before with trailer wheel chocks and reconnect the trailer to the car and the job is finished.

Often the towing vehicle will be on a dirt or unfirm surface. If the wheels of the towing vehicle start to dig in or skid during retrieval, stop immediately. Attempting to pull the trailer out will only worsen the situation. The sand or dirt can be scooped away from the wheels and the traction increased by laying down some boards or tire chains. If that doesn't work detach the boat trailer and slowly give gas to the towing vehicle, trying not to spin the wheels until solid ground is reached. Then attach a rope or chain from the towing vehicle to pull the trailer to solid ground. Another helpful hint when launching through sandy or soft areas is to deflate the tires of both the car and trailer about 5 pounds. If launching in such areas is common, carry a tire pump or pressure cylinder for emergency flats to refill the tires after deflating.

TRAILER TONGUE EXTENSIONS

Some trailer manufacturers offer a trailer tongue extension as an option. The trailer frame is made with a larger rectangular central tongue. A smaller tube fits closely inside and pulls out for launching and retrieval. The extension places the tow vehicles driving wheels further from the water to provide better traction. A tongue extension is advantageous for gentle launching slopes or when the boat must have deep water to float off of the trailer. The towing vehicle driving wheels can be kept clear of the water's edge, where the ramp is most often quite slippery.

how to build boat trailers

A wood or metal tongue extension that does not rigidly fasten to the trailer can also be used for launching or retrieving a trailer. FIG. 14-3 illustrates such a device that has a coupler on one end and a hitch on the other to couple the trailer to the towing vehicle. Backing up without a rigid connection to the trailer is difficult; the rig will tend to jackknife unless on a slope where the weight of the trailer will tend to lead the towing vehicle into the water.

HELPFUL HINTS

Some people use the power of the boat to assist in retreiving or launching the boat from the trailer. If the trailer becomes stuck in the bottom during retrieval and/or the towing vehicle is having a tough time pulling it out, the boat motor power can provide that little extra shove. The boat must be centered on the trailer by strong uprights as side drift could damage the motor's underwater appendages. The motor should be shut off as soon as practical so the water pump doesn't run dry, or the prop tends to cavitate or race.

A walkway along the trailer in fore and aft directions is a great help in both launching and retrieving. The walkway will enable you to pull or push the boat to the end of the trailer without getting waist deep in water. Be sure the walkway has a textured surface with non-skid deck paint, paste on strips, or carpeting to prevent slipping.

A trailer hitch mounted on the front of the towing vehicle is an excellent assist. This especially holds true if the towing vehicle has limited rear-view vision. With a front hitch, you clearly see what is taking place, and with a rear drive towing vehicle, the wheels are on solid, usually dry ground to provide better traction. ❖

TRAILER HANDLING

Towing a trailer behind a car or pickup truck is easy, providing common sense is used. Remember, the trailer tires will make a shorter arc than those of the towing vehicle when making a turn or negotiating a curve. Prior to making a turn, go straight for a while longer, then make a sharp turn. When you make a left hand turn or negotiate a turn to the left, stay as far to the right as practical and legal. Conversely when making a turn to the right, stay to the left as far as safely possible. Take curves smoothly; always remember you have a "tail" behind your towing vehicle.

If you must pass another vehicle, be careful. With the added weight, you are not going to have the acceleration that you would normally have. Never attempt passing unless you have completely clear lanes ahead. Watch your speed; and be very careful of the length of your vehicle, both in making the initial swing out, and again when cutting back into the lane, so that you don't collide with the passed vehicle.

If your trailer is not equipped with brakes, use extra caution in coming to a stop. The braking will require more distance, and if you slam on the towing vehicle's brakes too hard, the trailer is liable to jackknife. Make stops as slowly and gradually as is prudent and always leave more room to stop than seems necessary.

If the trailer is equipped with a separate brak-ing system not coupled to the car, use both the towing vehicle and trailer brakes to bring the rig to a stop. Don't use the trailer brakes only to slow down or stop, as such action creates a tremendous strain on the hitch.

It is imperative that a clear view of the trailer and the area behind it be maintained. Often the trailer width is more than that of the car, and the standard, small rear-view mirrors common to passenger vehicles, are not ad-equate. Special clamp on side-view mirrors that can be removed when not towing a trailer are available. Properly adjusted, they give a complete view to the rear of the trailer and are helpful not only when driving on the highways, but also when maneuvering the trailer in tight quarters.

BACKING A TRAILER

Many people have trouble controlling a trailer when backing up. Turn the car wheels to the right as you begin to back up and the trailer will turn left. Turn the wheel of your car to the left and begin backing up, and the trailer will swing to the right. A popular method of back-ing a trailer is to grip the towing vehicle steer-ing wheel at the bottom; moving the hand to the left makes the trailer go to the left and moving to the right makes the trailer go right.

A better view of the trailer is obtained by twist-ing the torso and looking over the right shoul-

how to build boat trailers

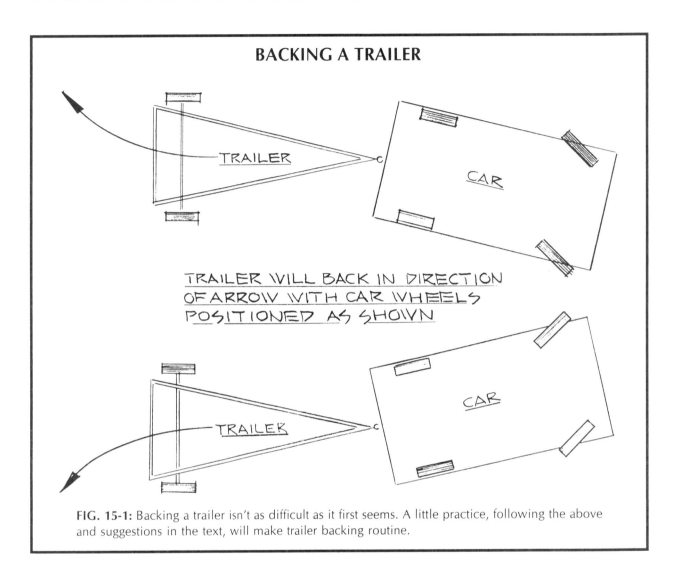

BACKING A TRAILER

TRAILER WILL BACK IN DIRECTION
OF ARROW WITH CAR WHEELS
POSITIONED AS SHOWN

FIG. 15-1: Backing a trailer isn't as difficult as it first seems. A little practice, following the above and suggestions in the text, will make trailer backing routine.

der thru the rear window. It's easier to back-up if the turn is started from the drivers left side and continues in a clockwise direction. Whenever possible, make your turn in this manner as the path of the trailer will be in easy sight in the drivers side view mirror. Practicing backing a trailer on an empty parking lot or open space will save many embarrassing moments. Controlling a trailer behind a tow vehicle is a knack and with practice, backing onto the launch ramp or parking spot will become second nature.

BE PREPARED

Anyone contemplating even a short trip with a boat trailer should be equipped for emergencies. A spare tire and/or a wheel is a must. No one should leave for a trip without a jack and lug wrench that will fit the trailer. The typical auto jack isn't worth much to lift a car, and it is almost impossible to use with a trailer; a good compact hydraulic jack is recommended. Don't forget flares or reflectors for emergencies such as changing a tire on a

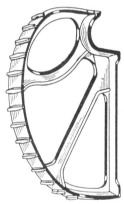

FIG. 15-2: A clever method to jack a trailer with a flat tire. Made from cast aluminum this device will rotate and raise the trailer from the ground when pulled by the towing vehicle.
Courtesy B & M Manufacturing

busy or narrow roadside.

All trailers should carry a selection of spare parts. An extra set of wheel bearings with an extra cotter key is a must. Some grease for re-packing the wheel bearings should accompany the bearings, and a grease gun if bearing savers are used. Electrical tape and a spare bulb for the lights are important in case of an electrical problem on the road.

A length of tow cable is also a desirable piece of equipment. Getting stuck in the sand is no fun, but a short length of cable attached to the towing vehicle from another car will frequently pull the rig out. Often, too, if the car can be moved to firmer ground, the cable can be used from the car to the trailer to tow the trailer clear. Don't be caught short. Start each trip by preparing for trouble. If something does happen and you are prepared, it isn't trouble, just routine.

An experienced trailer boater never starts even the shortest trip without double checking the entire trailer and tow vehicle. You have too much investment in your rig to overlook this procedure. The ball hitch on the trailer should be inspected to be sure it is tight, clean and lightly oiled. The coupler should be tightened then bumped a few times, re-tightened, and re-checked to be sure the locking mechanism is operating. Inspect the trailer safety chain connections. The lighting system should be completely tested to be sure all systems are ready to use. Check the air pressure in the tires. Make sure the boat is positioned correctly and all hold downs are tight. Check any gear in the boat and be sure it won't move. Each time you come to a stop for gasoline or a bite to eat, inspect each of the above and the wheel bearings to be sure they aren't overheating.

We hope this book will help make towing a boat and trailer to launching sites pleasurable, the launching and retrieving go smoothly, and each boating excursion more fun than the preceeding one. ❖

Appendix

The following are sources for information concerning products mentioned in this book.

Atwood Mobile Products — 4750 Hiawatha Dr., Rockford, IL 61103

B & M Manufacturing — 7643 Old Lamar Ave. (Old Hwy 78), Olive Branch, MS 38654

Dexter Axle — 222 Collins Rd., Elkhart, IN 46515

Draw-Tite, Inc. — 40500 Van Born Rd., Canton, MI 48188-2999

Dutton-Lainson Company — 451 W. Second St., Hastings, NE 68901

Fulton Performance Products — 50 Indian Head Dr., Mosinee, WI 54455

Powerwinch — 100 Production Dr., Harrison, OH 45030

TAP (Trailer Adaptable Products) — 502 2nd St., Unit 1, Berthoud, CO 80513

Trailer Boat Magazine — 20700 Belshaw Ave., Carson, CA 92704

Trail-Rite — 3100 W. Central, Santa Ana, CA 92704

Unique Functional Products (Bearing Buddy) — 135 Sunshine Ln., San Marcos, CA 92069

Index

Index

Index

Other GLEN-L Publications

BOATBUILDING WITH PLYWOOD

BEST BOOK ON PLYWOOD BOATBUILDING. Index, hundreds of photos, drawings, illustrations, 312 pages, 8 1/2"x11" - Hardcover.

HOW TO FIBERGLASS BOATS

ANSWERS ALL YOUR QUESTIONS ABOUT FIBERGLASSING A PLYWOOD BOAT. Index, glossary, over 100 photos & illustrations, 128 pages, 8 1/2"x11" - Softbound.

INBOARD MOTOR INSTALLATIONS

HOW TO CONVERT AN AUTOMOTIVE ENGINE, INSTALL HARDWARE. Index, hundreds of photos, drawings & illus., 250 pages, 8 1/2"x11" - Hardcover.

FIBERGLASS BOATBUILDING FOR AMATEURS

COMPREHENSIVE REFERENCE FOR FIBERGLASS BOATBUILDING. Index, glossary, bibliography, 257 photos, 127 drawings, charts, tables, graphs, 400 pages, 8 1/2"x11" - Hardcover.

"GLEN-L BOOK OF BOAT DESIGNS"

A CATALOG OF BOAT PLANS, KITS, AND SUPPLIES AVAILABLE FROM GLEN-L. Illustrated, 176 pages, over 240 boat designs.

GLEN-L Videos

HOW-TO VIDEOS:

"HOW TO FIBERGLASS A BOAT"

DE-MYSTIFIES THE FIBERGLASSING PROCESS. One hour and 30 minutes.

"STITCH-N-GLUE BOATBUILDING"

A COMPLETE OVERVIEW OF STITCH-N-GLUE BOATBUILDING, FROM LAYING OUT THE PATTERNS TO FINISHED BOAT. One hour and 25 minutes.

VIDEOS DESCRIBING THE CONSTRUCTION OF THREE GLEN-L STITCH-N-GLUE DESIGNS:

"BUILDING THE CONSOLE SKIFF"

A 16' CENTER CONSOLE SKIFF, THE FISHERMAN'S DREAM. Thirty minutes.

"BUILDING THE SEA KAYAK"

LEARN HOW EASY IT IS TO HAVE YOUR OWN 17' TOURING KAYAK. Thirty minutes.

"BUILDING THE EIGHT BALL-SG"

AN 8' SAILING PRAM: SAILING TRAINER OR THE IDEAL DINGHY. Thirty minutes.